UPWARD ROAD

GoTo Publish

UPWARD ROAD

The Autobiography of Poet

DADISI MWENDE NETIFNET

Dadisi Mwende Netifnet
Visit my website at www.poetdadisi.com

Printed in the United States of America

 GoTo Publish

GoToPublish LLC
1-888-337-1724
www.gotopublish.com
info@gotopublish.com

In loving memory of my younger brother and best friend,

Edward (Gus) Alston.

May he rest in peace.

Other Books and CDs by Dadisi Mwende Netifnet

Think With Your Spiritual Mind (Spiritual poems)

Love Flows Like a River (Love poems)

Poetry for Today's Young Black Revolutionary Minds

A Bachelor's Wish List

Sick People: The Things We Rather Not Talk About

Had I Only known (Novel)

Need I Say More (Poetry)

CDs by the author that are on Spotify, itunes and Apple music.

My Cheating Days Are Through (Spotify playlist)

Humanity Speaks: Black Lives Matter (Spoken words to music, pt. 1 & 2)

Poetdadisi.com

CONTENTS

CHAPTER 1

In the Beginning

How my parents met is interesting to me. (To avoid confusion, I will refer to them by their first names.) In 1944, Anna Mae's parents, stepfather William and Eva Mae Rivers, were living in a boarding house at 584 King Street just across the street from the old famous Lincoln Theater in Charleston, South Carolina. Elijah often visited his sister, Essie Mae, and her husband in Charleston. Elijah lived in a small town outside of Charleston called Midland Park. On one of these visits, Eva asked Elijah if he had a lady friend. He smiled and responded that he did not. She told him, "I have five daughters; I'll introduce them to you one day."

Charleston was famous for its ice cream float celebration on King Street. On one hot and humid Sunday evening in June 1944, Eva and two of her daughters, Anna Mae and Loretta, were enjoying the festivities. Elijah spotted Eva and the girls in the crowd and made his way toward them. Eva introduced them and they started talking about the evening events. He noticed Anna Mae's lovely pink dress. Soon the conversation seemed to be between Elijah and Loretta only; Anna Mae had little to say. Eva said goodbye and left them alone with Elijah, which was a bold move in those days. While Elijah walked with them, they continued to talk. He was impressed with their good manners, their common sense, and the modest way they were dressed. Soon they reached their destination and bade Elijah goodbye. He said, "It was nice meeting you. I hope to see you again soon."

Two days later, just past supper time, Elijah passed the house again. Anna Mae was washing dishes and saw him through the kitchen window that faced the road. Her grandmother, Mrs. Simmons, was sitting on the front porch in her rocking chair smoking a pipe. Elijah climbed the porch steps and greeted her politely. "Evenin', son," she replied, adjusting the pipe between her lips.

"I've come to visit your granddaughter," he said.

"What for?" Grandmother Simmons snapped.

With nervous apprehension, he answered, "Only to talk."

"How do you know my granddaughters?" Grandmother Simmons asked sternly.

"I met them last Sunday at the festival. We spent the evening talking, and I thought I'd pay them a visit today if it's alright with you."

"Well, let's see if they want to see you. She called to them through the screen door and Loretta came out alone, casting furtive glances first at her grandmother and then at Elijah whom she had met only two days before. Grandmother Simmons asked, "Is this the one?"

Elijah replied, "Well, ma'am, I really wanted to talk to the tall one." Grandmother Simmons instructed Loretta to fetch her sister. Anna Mae came to the door, wiping her hands with a dish towel. "Is this the one?" Mrs. Simmons asked.

Remembering the pink dress, he replied, "Yes, ma'am." Mrs. Simmons leaned forward and peered at Elijah over her bifocals.

"If you want to talk to my granddaughter," she said, "then write me a letter asking permission." "Okay. Yes, ma'am," he said, nearly stumbling as he went down the porch steps. He hurried off to his sister's house on King Street to write his letter.

Anna Mae admired the young man's enthusiasm about writing the letter. Two hours later, he returned with the letter in hand. Mrs. Simmons was still sitting in her rocking chair on the porch when he arrived. "Evenin' boy. You back already?" He smiled and handed her the letter. She read it silently, placed it in her bosom, and then called Anna Mae outside. She looked thoughtfully at Anna Mae and then at Elijah. "All right, young man, you may talk to my granddaughter. If she's willing to keep company with you, be sure to take good care of her." She got up slowly, clasped her granddaughter's hand for a moment, and then went inside the house so that the two could be alone. Anna Mae never read the letter because of her grandmother's positive reaction. She knew it must have been something very special, and it won her heart.

Elijah and Anna Mae enjoyed a year of a whirlwind courtship. On a lovely Saturday on February 5, 1945, they were married at Grandmother Simmons' home. Elijah was twenty years old, Anna Mae sixteen.

In due time, my parents started their family. From their union came nine children. I was the seventh. I was told that my sisters, Miriam and Clarissa, claimed me as their very own. This was quite alright with Mama, because less than six months later, she was pregnant with her eighth child, Edward and later my baby sister Izetta.

My parents loved and lived together for 52 years until Daddy passed on January 2, 1999. I hope to follow in my father's footsteps as a committed husband and a good example to whatever children I may have.

My great-grandmother, Mamie J. Simmons, was born February 13, 1880; died April 27, 1979 at the age of 99.

CHAPTER 2

Starting School

I am the seventh of nine children born to Elijah and Anna Mae Alston. They are, in order of birth, Elijah, Jr., whom we called "Wonnie," Clifford, Miriam, Clarissa, Annette, and Mamie. I, Marvin, come next, followed by Edward ("Eddie") and Izetta. We lived at 105 Spring Street, Charleston, South Carolina. I was born on Saturday, April 11, 1959 at Medical College Hospital in Charleston. My mother gave her sister Grace permission to name me Marvin Leroy Alston, a name I later changed to an African name, Dadisi Mwende Netifnet.

Early one morning in September 1965, when I was six years old my mother woke me up and led me to the bathroom where she helped me bathe and get dressed in a beige shirt, brown pants, and brown shoes. I sensed that I was getting dressed up for a special occasion. Mama told me to join my other siblings at the breakfast table. She said, "Don't Marvin look good?" Smiling at me, they agreed.

"Why am I dressed up? Where I am going?" I asked.

"To school. This will be your first day. Remember I told you that last night?" Since I hadn't gone to kindergarten, I really didn't know what to expect in first grade. Miriam, ten years older than I, slid out of her chair and walked around the table to kiss me on the cheek. (I was told that, when I was a baby, she often fed and clothed me and played with me as if I were her own child.) Sensing my confusion, she explained, "School is a place where you learn things. You're going to be a smart, handsome little boy, and I'm going to miss my baby." Mama brought me a plate of grits, eggs and sausage, and a cup of orange juice. Miriam touched my hand, telling me to be a good boy at school, then went back to her seat to finish her breakfast. Wonnie, Annette and Mamie got up and went to the living room to retrieve their books. Mama gave each one a brown bag lunch, and off they went to school. Clarissa remained at the table, not planning to go to school because of an asthma attack the night before. "Mama's going to take me to the doctor when she gets back from taking you to school," she said. I was accustomed to her frequent breathing problems. Mama would usually spray something in her mouth to help her breathe, but sometimes the spray didn't help and she'd have to see a doctor to get some relief. Of all the children, she was the one who got ill most often.

Clifford, my second oldest brother, once told me that before I was born, the family lived in the Gatson Green housing projects. In these projects, a family was allowed a maximum of six children per three-bedroom apartment. Well, I was the seventh child born and my parents brought me home to the projects at 32-B Flood Street. Clifford admitted that he had not been too excited to see me at the time. A nosy neighbor reported my parents for having violated the six-children rule, and our family was evicted in November 1959. My father moved our family to an old run-down house on 208 Line Street that had so little heat in the winter that it was always cold. I was told that when Aunt Grace stopped by the house and saw how we were living she ran out of the house and told our grandmother and great-grandmother about our unhealthy conditions. They insisted that we all move in with them until my father could do better. We stayed with them at 59 Radcliffe Street for four years. Then we moved to 105 Spring Street because our family had gotten too big for our grandparents' house.

When Clifford was seventeen, he left home against my mother's wishes. She wanted him to stay until he finished high school. He promised he would finish no matter where he was. He moved to Atlantic City, New Jersey with his best friend Donkey and the Bostic family. Denouncing poverty, he said he would never again walk around with holes in his underwear, ragged t-shirts and run-down shoes. He was drafted into the Army in 1968. After a year in Vietnam he was honorably discharged and moved to New York City to live with Aunt Grace and her husband, Uncle Felix, and their son Jamie.

Neither of my parents had finished grade school. My father had great working skills, which he passed on to us, but neither parent was prepared to teach us ordinary information. I didn't know my alphabets and didn't know how to count or identify colors. My father also had a drinking problem and spent most of the money he earned to maintain his alcohol habit. On the weekends when his problem was worst, he and Mama often got into terrible fights because he had spent our food money at a local bar. She tried to solve the problem by sending two of my brothers to the front door of The Cigar Factory where he worked to take his check and bring it home before he could spend it. He caught on to this and sneaked out the back door to avoid them and went straight to the bar. I don't know how my mother managed with a drunken husband and nine children, including one who was asthmatic, but she did. Like many Black mothers, she was a superhero, a miracle woman.

After I finished my breakfast, Mama and I headed for all-Black Simonton Elementary School on Smith Street, a tall white building with many windows. Once inside, I saw children in the hallway crying. Several of them were pulling on their parents, pleading, "Please don't leave me!" Afraid of what was going to happen to me, I held on tightly to my mother's dress. We headed to the principal's office where there more screaming children. I wondered what kind of school this was that my mother had brought me to. She told a lady behind the counter that my name was Marvin Leroy Alston, giving her some papers. Then the lady gave my mother some more papers to fill out and pointed us to a line to get into. This line led into another crowded room. Mama filled out the papers as we slowly moved forward. When we got to the front, I saw a pretty lady in a nurse's uniform smiling at me and holding a long needle. My mother, seeing my fear, told me to be a big boy. The nurse said the needle contained medicine to keep me and the other children from getting sick and that it was not going to hurt me; it would just pinch a little. After Mama rolled up my left sleeve, the nurse rubbed my arm with some alcohol and then stuck me with the needle. It didn't hurt much, and I wondered why so many of the children were screaming. My mother then escorted me down the hall to the classroom of Mrs. Green, a stout lady with glasses and a big smile. Mama told me that Mrs. Green would be my teacher and that I had to listen to what she said. Mama then bent down to give me a hug and a kiss on my cheek, telling me she would pick me up after school. There were about 35 other children in the classroom, some of them running around hitting one another and playing. Others had their heads down on their desk, crying for their parents to take them home. Mrs. Green tried to console them the best she could. I sat in the seat the teacher pointed out to me and waited for the class to begin. I almost got into a fight with a boy name Rickey. I was told by a boy who said he was Rickey's cousin that Rickey was repeating the first grade because he had a behavior problem. I didn't know any of the kids in my class and felt very lonely and afraid.

I don't remember anything that happened that first day and was relieved when the school day ended, and Mama picked me up. She asked me how my first day went. "Terrible," I told her. "I don't want to ever go back," but of course I had to.

Mrs. Green could not spend ample time with individual students. Some of them already knew their alphabets, as well as colors and numbers, but I had a hard time understanding what Mrs. Green was trying to teach us. To make things worse, Rickey, whose desk was next to mine, kept trying to pick a fight with me. How I got promoted to the second grade, I don't have the slightest idea.

My brother Eddie started first grade the following year. He caught on fast. He learned the alphabets and taught me how to tell time. My new teacher assigned my class homework, which I didn't have a clue how to do. There was always so much going on in my house that nobody in the family had time to give me much help. Since Eddie was now in school, I went to school and came home with him instead of Mama. One day I got my report card. I don't recall what grades I got, but I certainly remember the ass-whooping I got from my mother. She had never whipped me before! When she attended the parent-teacher conference, she learned about all the fighting I was doing in class with Rickey. From then on, I went to my room after school every day and pretended I was doing my homework. What I was really doing was copying words that I couldn't pronounce from my books, which I didn't know how to read. But I loved the feeling of holding a pencil in my hand. Somehow that simple action made me fall in love with writing. It was fun even though I didn't know the meaning of the words I copied.

Since my grades did not improve, I continued to get a whipping with each report card. I knew that my mother loved me and wanted me to do better. However, I kept allowing myself to get distracted each day by the other students. I felt like the dumbest of all her children since I was the only one getting a whooping for a bad report card. I remember Eddie once getting a beating, but it wasn't for his grades; it was because he was misbehaving around the house. He and I decided to run away from home, but we had no idea where we would go. When Grandmother Eva heard about my whoopings, she told my mother to stop and to be patient with me. She said I would learn one day, and Mama would be proud of me. Mama listened to her advice and assigned Annette to help me with my schoolwork.

CHAPTER 3

A Real Job

As far back as I can remember, my family was a normal and close-knit family. In the old days, during the summer of 1968, everyone had nicknames. When I was eight years old my father called me "Big-head Johnny." Apparently, I looked like his first cousin Johnny, whom I had never met; nonetheless, whose big head I had obviously inherited. Several of us were inseparable. One was my brother Eddie, who was a year younger than me and one of my best friends. We had a buddy, George Coaxem, "Nut". He lived next door. Our front yards were joined. Then there were brothers, Spencer and Bunny. Their grandmother lived behind us on Cannon Street. We met in her backyard under a mulberry tree. Usually when people saw one of us, they saw all of us in spite of age difference. Eddie, the youngest was seven; I was eight, Nut and Spencer were nine and Bunny was ten.

In the course of a day, the five of us had a world of fun together. We ventured (by nearly any means) to get a few nickels in our pockets. We'd walk a mile if we knew there might be returnable soda and beer bottles that we could collect to cash in. After all, we were junk-food junkies, with ice cream, and candy habits to support. Sometimes the bottles didn't exactly belong to us, but we would take them anyhow. Steal them was more accurate, but we kept this theft a secret since our parents would certainly beat us if they ever found out.

One day a white man we knew approached us. He owned the gas station at the corner of Spring and Rutledge Avenue. He asked if we wanted summer jobs. *Jobs*? Real *work*? We were delighted, and our faces must have shown it. No one had ever taken us seriously before. For instance, we once offered to help Mr. Henry, a Black man we knew who a roofer was, but he said, "Naw, not today; you boys are too little to do this kind of work." He was certainly right, but we didn't know that.

This time was different. Mr. Charlie really was going to give us jobs! I wondered, though, if his gesture was meant to discourage our daily bottle raids. After all, he had been our victim, which we were sure he knew. Perhaps he thought that offering us jobs would stop us from stealing bottles for coins to spend on candy, but if that was his intention, he was mistaken. We had no intention of giving up this lucrative practice.

Assured that we really wanted to work, he told us to be at his station the next morning—Friday, between 8:15 and 8:30 a.m. It was now Thursday evening around 6:00 p.m. We had no idea what our jobs would involve, but the thought of getting paid on a regular basis was so exciting that we really didn't care. It was already August and the new school year was fast approaching. As we hurried home in the sweltering heat, we chattered about the new wardrobes we intended to purchase from one of the downtown department stores with our first paycheck. "Third grade," I shouted, "here I come. I'll have money in my pocket and I ain't gonna give a doggone soul a penny!"

My house had a huge front yard. All five of us kids loved to sit on our long cement stoop or play in the yard while the adults sat and gossiped about everything. After supper that evening, we gathered there to continue speculating on our new jobs. We figured we'd get about 65 dollars apiece each week. This was the dreams of young boys who had never held jobs and who could not *begin* to determine how much gas station work paid. We wished "Mr. Charlie" had told us what our pay would actually be, but we were hopeful.

Around nine or so that night, the adults began to go inside, making way for the big boys who would then come around trying to court my older sisters and their friends. On this night, instead of playing games with some of the older boys as we usually did, we retired for the night. A good night's sleep was essential if we were to get up early the next morning.

It was 8:00 o'clock the next morning when we strode importantly up to the gas station. To our surprise, the owner had not yet arrived to open up, so we sat down on the station's few outdoor chairs and made hopeful conversation.

"Maybe we'll be fixin' cars or changin' tires," Nut said.

Spencer looked over at him. "I'm runnin' the cash box. Watch and see!" Whatever our jobs would be, we were ready.

Finally, after a ten-minute eternity of anxious waiting, we heard a truck approaching. It was the owner. This was it! We were about to get our summer assignments, and the money would start rolling in. We jumped to our feet as he approached the door.

He greeted us as he passed. "Mornin,' boys."

"Mornin,' sir," we responded. He opened the door and stepped inside, saying over his shoulder, "Wait outside. I'll be back out."

We sat down again and waited. And waited. At 8:22, two other white men ignored us, and went inside. The door slammed shut loudly behind them. More waiting. Soon someone else approached. This time it was a Black man.

"Good morning, boys," he said cheerily. "Are you ready to work today?"

"Yeah," said Eddie. "We just wish that white man would hurry up and let us in." The Black man assured us, "He'll be with y'all shortly." Then he, too, disappeared inside. We grew impatient and began to whisper among ourselves.

"Why don't he hurry his butt up?" mumbled Nut. "I feel like kicking him in it for makin' us wait like this."

As soon as he spoke, the door opened. Our new boss smiled and said, "Come on in and let me show you around." We jumped up and followed him inside.

We got the grand tour. In the reception and waiting area, the linoleum was patchy and worn out. Four chairs lined the left wall. The snack machine, though shaky-looking and old, was full of cold drinks. We followed him farther into the establishment.

The owner made it a point to stop at the only bathroom in the station. He had us gather around. The sink was covered in grease and soap scum. Customers could wash their hands with the pieces of broken soap in a once-shiny silver dish. The crappy-smelling commode appeared to have never been introduced to any type of cleaning solution. Along with the smell, the dirty rings inside it made me want to gag. We glanced at each other, anticipating the dirty job he expected us to do. "Oh, no we ain't!' one of the boys whispered. "We didn't come here for this mess! We want to get paid, but we sure as hell ain't cleaning up *this* filth!" The owner did not tell us why he had paused so long there.

"C'mon," he said, leading us to the garage where we met two white mechanics who had come in earlier. They smiled and seemed glad to see us.

"You boys look really healthy and strong. Do a good job, OK?" one said.

"Yes, sir, you bet!" we agreed. *Now* we were getting somewhere. We started to relax then, thinking that we were being hired to work with them, helping to fix cars, repairing and changing flat tires and the like. But to our surprise, we were ushered right past the mechanics, out of the garage, and around to the back of the building.

Jesus! Where were we? What was this? Our thoughts were racing 150 miles an hour at least. The scenery had changed from the comfortable chairs at the neatly swept front entrance to the promise of cool drinks in the lobby, and on to the orderliness of the mechanics' area—to this. We stood in a weed-infested, overgrown jungle swarming with large noisy insects. The grass was taller than we were. We felt as though we had been zapped into a freak zone on another planet.

We gawked in amazement at our surroundings. We barely heard Mr. Charlie when he said, "O.K. boys, this is your job. I want the grass cut and the lot as clean as a whistle." He passed out some tools, and then turned and left us alone. None of us said a word, but our expressions as we looked at one another conveyed everything we felt. As if in a dream, we stumbled around in the dense overgrowth with the tools we had been issued, sometimes unable to see one another. I had a hoe, Nut and Bunny dragged shovels, and Spencer and Eddie had been given swing blades. Nut spoke up first.

"Cuttin' grass? Man, there ain't no money in doin' this." He slowly looked around. "I ain't cuttin' all this. He must be outta his mind." Spencer agreed. "I ain't working out here in this hot sun all day," he shouted. "I'm already Black enough as it is!"

Eddie, who always complained about hard work, didn't even *pretend* he was going to try. He didn't want anyone, especially the neighborhood girls, to see him "swinging no stupid swing blade like some kind of slave."

Bunny, on the other hand, had started digging up the ground. He was a boy who believed in working for his money, no matter what type of work was involved. I watched him for a minute and then decided to do a little work myself. I picked at the weeds every now and then using the hoe. Then I began working in earnest. Eventually, the others followed my lead. We worked until noon. So far, none of our pals had come around to investigate what we had been hired to do. We sort of expected that they might, after all the bragging we had done the night before. Somewhere off in the distance the noon whistle blew and 'Mr. Charlie' came outside. He said, "You boys take a thirty-minute break."

Thank God! We were just about to sit down under a tree to eat the lunches we had brought when we spotted my older sister Miriam walking down Spring Street. We darted behind the trees and hid, hoping she couldn't see us. She got to the corner and turned left, walking away from the gas station.

We knew that the street would soon be crowded, and everyone was going to see us slaving in the station's field. We could imagine them saying, "Is this what y'all sacrificed having fun last night for? Is this what y'all went to bed early for?" We could almost hear the older boys taunting us: "Damn fools!"

We all agreed that this was a low-down job for us, and one that we hated every moment of. With that, Bunny, Nut, Spencer, Eddie, and I decided to quit and walked off our first real job—without even getting paid.

When we arrived home, we sat on the stoop, disheartened. We all felt disappointed that we had not made any money. No one said anything, but I'm sure we were all thinking of the new school clothes that we wouldn't have now, and worst of all, we could forget about getting paid on a regular basis. It was depressing. Still, we believed that one day, somehow, we would find that pot of gold at the end of a rainbow.

Just when it seemed that all hope was lost, an older Black boy we didn't know came running through my front yard at full speed. There was no one chasing him. We watched from the porch as he ran, tightly holding a bag. It looked like the kind of bank bag I had seen on TV shows. Suddenly he tripped and fell, dropping the bag. Silver coins flew in every direction. The boy jumped up, grabbing the bag and whatever remained in it, and kept on running past the back of my house. He leaped over the fence onto Cannon Street and disappeared.

When the boy was out of sight, we ran out to the yard and began picking up handfuls of fifty-cent coins. I had never before seen coins that large or so many of them. This was the treasure we had dreamed of.

Later that evening, the boy came back looking for his money. We were inside Nut's house when he came into our backyard. We watched him from the window. None of us went out to talk to him. When he finally left, I put my hands in my pocket enjoying the feeling of our sudden wealth. Now we could buy new school clothes. In addition, we could eat a lot of good junk food that week.

None of us said anything about where the money came from, but in the back of our minds we knew from the boy's behavior that it had to have been stolen. Nobody mentioned that we had no right to keep the coins or that the right thing to do would be to report it and give it to the police or some other official to return to the rightful owner. Nor did we discuss letting our parents know about our stolen wealth. We were so happy to get the money, and at that point, our knowledge of right and wrong never entered our minds.

We were sitting on Nut's porch when he told us to wait a minute as he ran into his house to get a small knife. When he came back outside, we followed him behind my house. He made a small cut on his right thumb until it began to bleed. He passed the knife for each of us to make a small cut on our right thumbs until we saw blood. He then instructed us to make a circle. He then got into the middle of the circle and press his bloody thumb against each one of ours. Then each one of us took turn stepping in the middle of the circle and pressing our bloody thumb against each other. Nut said that it was symbolic that we were blood brothers for life.

CHAPTER 4

Brothers and Sisters

Growing up, we lived in a small house at 105 Spring Street. The house had only two large bedrooms, but somehow, we were able to make do with nine children and two adults, and no one ever slept on the living room couch. Mama was a master at budgeting the family's money, delegating responsibilities, and teaching us to share. As little as we had, she would often say, "Whatever you have, be willing to part with it to help someone else; you never know when you yourself might be in need."

Mama was an excellent cook. On Sundays, our friends were always welcome to come to dinner, and the house was always crowded. After dinner we kids would often walk downtown to window shop, visit Colonel Lake, and stop by The Battery, Charleston's waterfront. When we returned home, we knew that we would have delicious desserts—ice cream, cakes, pies, peach cobbler, and bread pudding or banana pudding.

During the week Daddy worked at the cigar factory in Charleston. On weekends he took care of the lawns and gardens for several rich white people. Mama didn't have a job outside the home, but occasionally she did day work for the families Daddy worked for on weekends to make some extra money. Daddy believed that he and the children should go to bed early so that we would get enough sleep and be alert for the next day's activities, so my most vivid memories are things that happened on weekends or in the summer.

Eventually, Miriam joined Clifford in New York and got a job in a downtown department store. In November of 1967, Clifford was drafted into the U.S. Army to fight in the Vietnam War. My eldest brother "Wonnie" had long ago left home to get married. He and his wife Betty were raising a family, and he was now a minister. In Miriam's absence, Clarissa was in charge, taking on some of the duties herself and assigning others to the rest of the children to help Mama. For Christmas Miriam bought new clothes for Eddie, our baby sister Izetta, and me; she bought clothes for school and church. Clifford bought Eddie and I wagon wheels. Now Mama wouldn't have to buy them.

In the fall, she bought new school and church clothes for Eddie, our baby sister Izetta, and me. Now, Mama wouldn't have to buy them.

Although I missed my brothers, I enjoyed having Clarissa in charge. She was like a second mother to me. I felt comfortable discussing all of my problems with her; she would always listen, give her best advice, and treat me with kindness.

My third sister, Annette, took on the job of always keeping our house spotless. Like Clarissa, she made sure that all of us pitched in and did our part. Annette is an Aries, just like Mamie and me, and I have always felt close to her. Our birthdays are just two days apart. Annette was born April 7th, Mamie, on April 9th, and I was born on the 11th.

Generally, Annette was a beautiful person with a very nice personality. The trick to helping her stay that way was to never, ever make her angry.

When she became angry, she would become as ferocious as a lion straight from the African jungle. One Saturday morning, Annette woke up in a bad mood. It was close to 10 o'clock in the morning and she wanted me to get up so that she could make up my bed. "I don't feel like getting up," I mumbled. "It's too early. I'll clean my room myself." That wasn't good enough; she insisted on getting her chores done early and had no intention of letting me cause her delay. Half asleep, I scoffed, "I'll get up when I'm ready. Get out of my room."

The next thing I knew, I felt strong fingers clamping down on my right arm. She jerked me completely out of bed. She wasn't going to let her little brother tell her what to do. I was still savoring the idea of sleep and became absolutely furious that she had snatched me awake. I knew right then that we were going to get into it. Not that this was unusual; we got into tussles regularly. Every now and then, we even fought like cats and dogs. Mama must have heard the noise but didn't interfere. Annette was the cat, but today this dog wasn't going to stand for being beaten. Maybe it was a sibling power thing I don't know. Annette threw me against the wall like a rag doll. I guess all that cleaning had made her stronger than I realized. I screamed. Clarissa came running to my rescue. She knew that once Annette got started, it would be hard to get her to stop. While the two traded words, I dashed into the bathroom sniffling and began to get dressed while Jackie cleaned my room. So much for defending my hide.

As it turned out, I missed breakfast that morning. Later in the evening, Annette apologized for the ordeal. She prepared my dinner and placed it in the oven to warm. She seldom bore a grudge; we usually let bygones be bygones. She and I spent the rest of the evening playing hide-and-seek and telling silly stories.

Although we had our share of fun, my sisters often got tired of having to take us everywhere they went. Mama always took little Izetta with her to her Friday night club meeting, leaving Eddie and me with Clarissa, Annette, and Mamie (the hilariously funny one). The girls frequently protested but only under their breath. It was Annette who, on one occasion (and only one), finally spoke up. She complained to Mama. "I don't see why we always have to drag Marvin and Eddie along whenever we go somewhere. They're not *our* children. *We* didn't have them."

Mama calmly responded, "First of all, young lady, I'm going to my club meeting, and you know it's going to be too hot for those boys to be sitting in that clubhouse. On top of that, they have nothing to do. Why don't you want to take them with you? What are you doing that you don't want them to see? And by the way, Annette, it seems to me you're the only one complaining."

"It's embarrassing," Annette muttered.

Mama had stayed calm long enough. "Who do you think you talking to, gal?" she shouted. "You must think you're talking to one of those floozies in the streets, 'cause I *know* you can't be talking to *me* like that!"

Annette sucked her tongue against her teeth. What did she do that for? Mama yelled at her as if she wanted to pop her in the mouth.

Annette hollered, "But Mama!" It wasn't what she had said as much as what she had done. Sucking your teeth was like saying "what-*ever*," is considered a major sign of disrespect, especially if you're talking to your mother.

"'But Mama,' nothing. If you *ever* suck your teeth at me again, I'll knock them out." Mama turned and walked away. Annette stormed into the girls rooms where she stayed until Mama left that evening.

When Annette finally came out, her eyes were still red from crying. Eddie and I began laughing at her. We wanted her to know that we were glad Mama had put her in her place, especially since she bossed us around all day. I saw that the look in her eyes had changed, and I stopped laughing. Eddie, who liked to tease, kept on laughing. Annette's eyes were growing angrier; that African lion was emerging again. She marched straight over to Eddie and pushed him. He stumbled backwards a few steps.

"Leave me alone," he said. "I'm gonna tell Mama on you when she comes home!"

Annette seemed determined to get revenge on someone for how Mama had made her feel. She pushed Eddie again. This time, he pushed her back. Annette grabbed Eddie by the shirt and then it was on; they started fighting. Eddie screamed, "Let me go! I'm telling Mama!"

Just then the kitchen door opened and in walked Clarissa. As I've said, Clarissa was like a second mother and was always kind to me. She may not have enjoyed having us constantly tagging along, but I never got tired of being with her. And now, once again, she was right on time. She came to the rescue, shaking her head in an oddly grown-up manner as she separated her siblings. Annette gave in. She knew better than to mess with Clarissa; it would be a fight she would not win. The incident was over.

◆ ◆ ◆

In the 1970s, Clarissa and Annette were pom-pom girls at Burke High School. When they were not at one of their school's games on weekends, they were cheering for the boys of Michelle Park. While they cheered, Eddie and I played on the merry-go-round and the swings. After the game we would all go to the dance hall.

I could hardly wait for the weekends to come around because weekends with my sisters were fun. By now, they seemed to enjoy having us with them. At nighttime Eddie and I, my sisters, and the whole gang would sit on the long cement stoop in front of our house. We begged for nickels and dimes from the people coming out of the Ice House Company across the street. Each of us would take a turn running across the street to get change whenever an adult would offer it. We took what we collected to the corner and asked an adult to buy us a box of fried chicken from the bar. The music from the bar jammed with the Motown sound, and we'd be dancing in the street.

Later, we would hurry to the dance at Gage Hall to party. By this time, Clarissa was dating Eddie, her friend Sandy's brother. Annette was dating his brother Mink. My sisters were well known at Gage Hall. Although we were young, they had no trouble getting their little brothers into the building. I'm pretty sure the manager there understood their child-care situation.

Once inside, we could count on the fellows to buy us soda pops. They wanted to get on our good side in order to flirt with Carolyn and our neighbors, Barbara Ann and Connie, who were sisters. Their philosophy was, "If a guy ain't cute, I don't want a damn thing to do with him." The girls didn't seem to require attention or affection from any of the boys. They simply wanted to dance and have a good time. Clarissa and Eddie were always carrying on in a lovey-dovey manner. You could find them seated in a dark corner of the dance hall, gazing into each other's eyes.

Eddie and I sat in our favorite corner near the pop machine. We were just kids watching the world of grown-ups. We'd whisper, "Look, look!" when we spotted one of the fellows rubbing his hand across a girl's behind during a slow song. We'd laugh and laugh from our little corner.

Occasionally an older girl would grab one of us and make us dance with her. Thinking it was normal (or at least expected), we would rub a hand on her bottom as we had seen the older fellows do. Sometimes there was no reaction, but every now and then, one of them would hit us on the arm and then go back and tell our sisters how nasty we were behaving. Clarissa or Annette would sometimes scold us, but our neighbor, understanding those girls' *secret* reactions, would say to one or another of them, "Girl, please; you know you like it."

When I was out with my sisters on the weekends, the only thing I dreaded was going home. Mamie got a kick out of scaring us, and she often succeeded. The later and darker it was, the scarier it seemed. One Saturday night we were leaving our aunt's house where we had gone to hang out with our cousins. As we walked down Rutledge Avenue, then across Radcliffe Street, Mamie told one of her mystery stories. That night, it was about a woman she called "The Hag." She said, "The Hag hid in dark alleys, waiting for little boys so that she could take them out to the railroad tracks and "ride their behinds all —night— long." Suddenly, Mamie stopped walking. She stood stock still, as if she was listening for something. We stood still, too, eyes wide, waiting. After a few seconds, she began walking faster, saying, "I hear someone following us, and if it's the Hag, I'll be doggone if I'm going to let her ride my little brothers' behinds all night." She bent down, picked up a rock, and then turned and threw it.

Suddenly, she grabbed Eddie by the hand shouting, "Oh, God! Oh, God! A hag is on Marvin's back!" My sisters started running, shouting over and over that The Hag had gotten hold of me. Although I didn't feel anything on me, I screamed bloody murder and ran like the dickens. My heart felt as if it was going to burst, especially after I saw a porch light come on and a strange-looking woman started hollering and screaming from an ugly-looking house.

When we finally arrived home, everyone was bent over, breathing hard, and laughing uncontrollably—everyone, that is, but me. Mamie told me that she only pulled the stunt so that I would walk faster. She wanted to make sure we got to the house before Mama came home. Clarissa explained that the woman on the porch was hollering because Mamie had thrown the rock that landed too close to her for comfort. I felt like beating her up for scaring me so, but I knew she would never allow that! She adored her little brothers. Eventually, I started laughing myself as I remembered how gullible I had been to fall for her prank and to be so afraid of something that didn't exist. Someday, I vowed, I would play the same trick on someone else.

CHAPTER 5

The End of Racial Ignorance

History books record the events of the turbulent 1960s, but I was unaware of the violence that erupted throughout the country until I began to experience things for myself. On Mother's Day, May 14, 1961 a bus carrying Freedom Riders through Alabama was bombed. On June 12, 1963 NAACP field secretary Medgar Evers was murdered in his front yard in Mississippi by a white leader of the Ku Klux Klan. On November 22 of the same year President John F. Kennedy was assassinated while riding in a motorcade in Dallas, Texas. Two years later, on February 21, 1965 Malcolm X was assassinated in Manhattan's Audubon Ballroom just before he was scheduled to make a speech. Three years later, on April 4, 1968, Dr. Martin Luther King, Jr. was assassinated on the balcony outside of his room at the Lorraine Motel in Memphis, Tennessee. Presidential candidate Robert F. Kennedy was shot three times shortly after midnight on June 5 at the Ambassador Hotel in Los Angeles; he died on June 6, 1968. Riots in cities like Washington, D.C., Chicago, Detroit 1967, and the Watts area of Los Angeles exploded in 1968. These are just a few examples of the violence of the 1960s, which I learned about later.

In 1968 and 1969, events came closer to home. Charleston, South Carolina became the hotbed for the Civil Rights Movement. Black activist Mary Moultrie was a nurse's aide at Medical College Hospital, but the hospital refused to honor her licensed practical nurse certification. She and 400 co-workers led a strike for better working conditions and pay for Black people at the hospital. Reverend Ralph Abernathy, Coretta Scott King, Andrew Young, Hosea Williams, and thousands of other Black people assisted them in a march against the state hospital for better wages. There was also a demand in New York City for union jobs for African Americans.

The Civil Rights activities that took place in Charleston in March, 1969 were a rude awakening for this little ten-year-old boy. Late one afternoon my mother hurried my brother Eddie and me out the house and headed down Spring Street. I didn't understand the rush. It was hard for us to keep up with her. When we reached the corner of Cannon Street and Ashley Avenue we stopped and waited. For what, I didn't know. I could hear the faint sound of music. An elderly Black woman saw us and invited us to come upstairs with her and stand on her balcony to view "the march." I didn't know what "the march" meant and was still unaware of what was about to take place until the lady told us to look far down the street to the left. I could not believe my eyes. There were thousands of Black people headed our way. The music I'd heard was the sound of their songs. As the marchers got closer their singing grew louder and louder, *We ain't gon' let nobody turn us around!* I had never in my life seen so many Black people in one place at one time. There were some white people in the march too. Mama pointed out a Black man at the front of the crowd. "That's Reverend Ralph Abernathy," she said. I thought he had a fat head. It's funny what minor details kids notice. I saw many of my classmates among the marchers.

They had skipped school to help our people in the struggle. I begged Mama to let me join them but she refused. She was afraid I might get hurt. Then I saw my sisters.

"Look, Mama! There's Clarissa! And there's Annette and Mamie too. Let me go with them," I pleaded. "I want to be an activist too! Clarissa will look out for me." But Mama would not change her mind. She was concerned for my safety and thought I would be in the way. She explained that the marchers were trained to know what to do if anything went wrong.

The march ended two hours later. Mama thanked the lady for letting us share her balcony. Walking home, I asked Mama where all those people were going. She said they were going over to the Morris Brown AME Church to hear the speakers. She went on to say that over 400 Medical College workers had elected a Black woman named Mary Moultrie as president of the district. The workers wanted union recognition, but the white establishment did not want the union involved in South Carolina's state jobs. Moultrie had invited SCLC leaders to assist her with the march. That was one year after Rev. Dr. Martin Luther King, Jr. was killed.

My sisters came home later that evening and told us about the events at the church. Annette explained to me that the march was to help gain better working conditions and higher pay for the Black employees in Medical College Hospital in Charleston. She said that our people were excited about ending segregation at the hospital and in many other places in Charleston.

Our People. Segregation. Unions. White establishment. Whites against Blacks. These new terms marked the beginning of my loss of social innocence. At ten years old I was learning the true nature of my world. I began to understand that there was a power structure and that our people weren't in it.

I was in the fifth grade at the time. I attended Mitchell Elementary School. The next day hardly any of my classmates came to school. My history teacher, Mr. Adams, explained that most of the students were probably marching with their parents. I asked if I could go downtown on King Street where another march was to start. He said no, that school was officially in session. It must have been about 11:00 a.m. when I heard the marchers in song again. I jumped up and ran to the window. Fishburne Street was filled with Black people marching. They appeared to be headed towards Burke High School. The sight of the marchers thrilled me. They were so determined to fight for freedom for us. There were so many students! I was exhilarated to see kids my own age fighting for their rights. The marchers were singing, *"We Shall Overcome."* I could not understand why I was being held back by both my mother and my history teacher. After the marchers disappeared and their singing faded, I cried. At that moment, I hated school again. I wanted desperately to rebel like the other students.

My older sisters' attitudes about life were changing. They had also been shaken out of innocence into a new reality of the world we had been born into. They became friends of a group called the Line Street Stompers. They began to wear their hair in the Afro style. They talked about Black people being brothers and sisters. They held their heads high and emphasized the need for respect and Black unity. They wore blue jeans with matching jackets. They looked good. They looked important. Eddie and I, getting older, did not hang around them too much anymore; we had our own friends now. Besides, our sisters were very busy activists now. We were proud of them.

The soulful songs of the 1960's and '70's touched me deeply. Songs like *"We Shall Overcome,"* by Charles Albert Tindley; *"Say It Loud (I'm Black and I'm Proud)"*, by James Brown, *"Keep on Pushing"*, by the Impressions, *"If You're Ready (Come Go with Me)"*, a song written by Curtis Mayfield and sung by The Staple Singers, *"Respect"*, sung by Aretha Franklin, written by Otis Redding and *"A Change Is Gonna Come"*, by Sam Cooke. These were just a few of the songs that kept Black people fired up in the struggle. Although Mama did not prevent the girls from participating in the Civil Rights Movement (commonly called "The Struggle"), she continued to refuse to let Eddie and me participate. She kept telling us we were too young to mingle in grown folks' affairs. I made up my mind then that when I grew up, I would be involved in the liberation struggle of Black people—by any means necessary.

CHAPTER 6

Porgy and Bess

There were only two teachers that I can recall in elementary school who cared whether or not I learned anything. One was Mrs. Annette McKenzie Anderson, a speech therapist at A. B. Rhett Elementary School. Twice a week she picked me up from my homeroom class and took me to her small office to teach me phonics and how to use my tongue to enunciate correctly.

The year was 1970 and I was in the sixth grade. I grew to love this teacher. She was helping me to rise to the same level as the other students in the sixth grade. However, after a year and a half Eddie and I were taken out of A.B. Rhett and transferred to Julian Mitchell School because the principal said we now lived in another school zone. Our family had indeed moved to a bigger house with three bedrooms at 176 Fishburne Street, two blocks from both schools. My mother wanted us to remain at A. B. Rhett because some of her other children had gone there; she felt we would get a better education there, but her protest did no good. The thought of going to a new school made me miserable. I would have to leave all my friends and try to make new ones.

One of the first students I ran into at Mitchell was Hubbie with whom I was constantly fighting. He, too, had been transferred from Rhett. We were in the same classroom though he was a year older than me. My mother and his mother were such good friends that Hubbie and I were considered cousins. Hubbie was just as much a class clown as I was. Now and then, for no reason, he would pick a fight with me calling me a Black Chinese. My classmates could not understand why we were always fighting since we were considered cousins. I already had enough problems concentrating on learning to have to deal with fighting too. I would go home and tell my mother on Hubbie. She would call his mother to ask her to tell him to stop picking fights with me. This went on for a while, but we finally stopped fighting.

At the end of the school year I was socially promoted from one grade to the next. My mother went to school and complained to the teachers for promoting me when I had not done well enough to go to the next grade. She argued that they were educationally crippling me, but her protests did no good.

Mr. Williams was my sixth and seventh grades homeroom teacher. He was also my math teacher. He made school bearable for me. He was fun and very easygoing. He often kidded me about my classroom clowning. I clowned because school was a joke to me. I only attended because my mother would put good use to an extension cord if I tried to drop out. Therefore, I had to make the best of an excruciating situation. However, I did meet Larry Polite, Darcy Phatt, Anthony Bradley, Joseph Newton and Slede Green among other guys who would become my lifelong friends.

My mother knew I hated school; it was evident on my report card. I received C's, D's and F's. I was the most academically challenged of all my siblings. Nevertheless, I was never retained in any grade although I was eventually placed in the special education program through the twelfth grade. Special Ed classes were not too challenging for me, and I began making better, passing grades.

Mr. Williams told me that if I was going to be a clown, I might as well make money at it. He said that a famous play called *Porgy and Bess* was going to be produced at our school and that students had a chance to audition for parts. One day, at the end of the school day, he called Eddie and me into his classroom. He told us that auditions for the play would take place that day in the auditorium and that we should try to get parts. Eddie got excited and told him we certainly would, but I was very hesitant because I didn't even know what a play or an audition was. Mr. Williams explained it to me; so, I went with him and Eddie to the auditorium. There I saw many other people, including adults and children. Some were waiting for their time to audition while others were already singing and reading various parts. All the schools in town were still racially segregated, but I saw one white lady there who seemed to be in charge. I was told that her name was Mrs. Ella Gerber and she would be directing the play. It seems that a writer for the *Charleston Evening Post* once wrote, "Mrs. Ella Gerber is a professional director and has supervised more than a dozen productions of *Porgy and Bess* all over the world since 1958."

I noticed Rochelle, who was in Eddie's class and one of our best friends, waving us over to sit with him. We moved to where he was sitting and watched each act. Up to this point the only people auditioning were adults, several of whom I recognized. I felt more at ease sitting with someone we knew.

At one point, Mrs. Gerber stopped the auditions to tell the children who were waiting what the play was about. She explained that Porgy was a crippled Black beggar who rolled along on a wooden wheel placed under his knees, and that he was in love with a beautiful Black woman named Bess. They lived in a slum of Charleston called Catfish Row.

After the adult auditions were over, it was announced that my speech therapist from Rhett School, Mrs. Annette McKenzie Anderson, was selected to play the role of Bess. I was very happy for her. Mr. Ruben Wright, a music supervisor at Sanders-Clyde Elementary School, got the role of Porgy. Then the director called the children up front for our auditions. There were about twenty kids, including Rochelle, Eddie and me. Everyone was instructed, one at a time, to skip and sing, "Crown cock-eyed drum, you can't tell dice from watermelon."

To our delight, Rochelle, Eddie and I, along with some other children, were chosen for parts. We were elated. Everyone was congratulating those who had been chosen. We were proud that the setting of the play was our hometown, Charleston, and that it was being produced there. I thought that I could finally quit school and become a star actor at the age of eleven, but it turned out that I had to go to school as usual. Mr. Williams was delighted about my part in the play. He and my classmates praised me for what seemed like forever. They nicknamed me "Little Porgy" and my classmate, Renee Harvey, "Bess." Renee didn't know it, but I was completely in love with her. She was short and pretty; I loved her more than I loved sunshine. When we shared the good news at home, the family was happy for Eddie and me.

We rehearsed daily after school and on Saturday afternoon for months. We rehearsed wherever Mrs. Gerber directed us to go. However, before the grand opening night we rehearsed at the newly-built Charleston Municipal Auditorium. During these rehearsals, I overheard some of the adult discussions and found out more about the play and its history. I learned that *Porgy and Bess* was first written as a novel and later as a play, both called *Porgy*, by DuBose Heyward, a white *Charlestonian*. George Gershwin read the play in 1926 and, after a visit to Charleston, proposed that he and Heyward collaborate in rewriting the play as a folk opera called *Porgy and Bess.* Gershwin composed the music and Heyward and Ira Gershwin wrote the words in 1934. It was first performed in New York City in 1935 with an all-Black cast. In 1959, the year I was born, *Porgy and Bess* was made into a film.

The night of our performance was full of excitement. Everyone in the cast was bubbling with energy. We were going to be stars in the eyes of thousands of people! When I got a chance, I peeked out from behind the curtain. All I could see were hundreds of faces. Beautifully dressed Black and white people of all ages filled the auditorium. Suddenly, the sight of so many people frightened the hell out of me! I ran to the back of the stage where Eddie and Rochelle were to tell them what I saw. They told me take a deep breath and relax. Eddie asked me if I had seen Mama and the girls. I hadn't. Eddie, who was eager to know how many people were in the audience, had already looked through the curtain. He said he had seen our mother and sisters high up in the balcony. I ran back to the curtain to look again and there they were, sitting upstairs in the balcony looking real pretty.

Minutes later, the cast came together, dressed up in an array of colorful 1930's costumes. I wore fashionable pink pants, a pink shirt, and white patent-leather shoes. We gathered around Mrs. Gerber and an elderly Black preacher said a prayer. After that, we all went to our positions, telling each other to "*break a leg.*"

There was so much activity on Catfish Row! Suddenly, the big band began to play. Colorful lights came on. The curtains opened. The adult actors and actresses stepped grandly onto the stage, ready to entertain the audience with this ever-popular story of love and drama.

I was really excited as I ran across the stage with the other children! We began running and skipping around the character Crown singing, "Crown cock-eyed drum, you can't tell dice from watermelon!" Crown prepared to engage in a deadly fight with Porgy. However, Sportin' Life, the drug dealer, came and rescued Bess, taking her away with him to New York City.

The applause of the audience made me feel like a star. Performing on the stage in *Porgy and Bess* was one of the most important moments of my youth. Judging by the laughter and applause of the audience, it was clear that everyone had done a beautiful job singing, dancing and acting. When the curtain finally closed, the crowd went wild. To a standing ovation, we came out from behind the curtain to bow at least five times. Someone told me later that the mayor of Charleston and other dignitaries from throughout South Carolina were in the audience.

After the play, the cast was told to go to the front lobby to greet the people who had attended. I didn't realize that even *my* autograph would mean so much to so many people. I felt like a celebrity. Suddenly, I spotted my homeroom teacher, Mr. Williams, in the crowd. I hurried over to him and, with a huge smile, I thanked him for introducing my brother and me to *Porgy and Bess*. It had truly been a great educational experience for me. He hugged me and introduced me to his wife and two young sons. Then, firmly shaking my hand, he smiled and said, "Marvin, you can do whatever you put your mind to. I am very proud of you. Keep it up, son." Moved by his word, I thanked him.

When I turned to leave I saw my former speech therapist, Mrs. Annette McKenzie Anderson, surrounded by autograph-seekers. She saw me as I walked toward her. "Marvin, you did a good job up there on stage. I am so very happy for you." She hugged me and looked at me intently. "You are destined for greatness," she told me. I thanked her and said, "You did a good job, too, Bess. Then I walked away to sign more autographs.

After receiving what seemed like endless hugs and kisses from our mothers and sisters backstage, Eddie, Rochelle, and I went down to the ballroom. There we ate a variety of delicious foods, including steak. We were not allowed to drink champagne, but we convinced some of the nice waiters to sneak us some champagne in a cup. One of our male friends in the cast had promised Rochelle's mother and mine that he would take us home after the reception. I drank so many cups of champagne that I got sick to my stomach and had to run to the restroom. We went home drunk that night. I'm eternally glad that my mother was asleep and never knew our condition.

The play ran from June 25 through July 8, 1970. It got rave reviews in the local newspapers. The day of the children's photo shoot I missed out. I must have been running around somewhere in the big auditorium. All the same, I am proud to report that my name was clearly listed on the program: *Marvin Leroy Alston.* All of our friends were very proud of us at school and in our neighborhood. At the end of the play that summer, Eddie and I each received a check for $100.00. Considering all the work we had put in, not to mention the hours, we felt somewhat cheated. Nevertheless, my mother took us shopping downtown, and with our hard-earned money we bought ourselves new clothes to wear back to school. And for once, I actually liked school.

CHAPTER 7

Shoeshine Boy

I was never good at sports. I tried to play little league baseball, but I didn't make the team. I tried to play basketball with my brothers and friends but wasn't good at that, either. One thing I *did* know how to do was make money. Once Eddie and I were too old to hang around with our older sisters we were free to do whatever we liked, as long as we first took the dirty clothes to the laundromat for my sisters to wash. The laundromat was right across the street from Mitchell Park. There my brother got even more involved with sports. My family had just moved to 176 Fishburne Street, a much bigger house.

Just down the street from our house on the corner of Rutledge Avenue and Fishburne Streets was a drugstore. Mama often sent me to buy medical supplies for the family. I was always friendly with the white owner there. One day he asked me if I wanted a job delivering prescriptions. The job would be after school, but I would need a bicycle. Daddy had several bicycles since we didn't have a car and that was his means of transportation. I told my parents about my job offer. They agreed and Daddy promised to lend me one of his bikes until I could buy my own.

I was twelve years old at the time and happy with my new job. With my salary of fifteen dollars a week, I was able to pay for my haircuts and my brother's as well. I also bought myself new tennis shoes. I would have bought my brother a pair, but he always wanted expensive ones. We had different tastes; he wanted only name-brand clothes. To me it didn't matter what brand it was as long as I liked it. I used the money I made in tips to buy candy for my sisters. I felt really grown- up delivering prescriptions all over the city on Daddy's bike often going to parts of the city I had never seen before.

I gained a new interest in the historic city of Charleston. Charleston was once called the *"Holy City."* However, nothing was holy about this city that enslaved thousands of African people for nearly 200 years. According to history, during the Transatlantic Slave Trade, Charleston was one of the busiest port cities in the nation for importing Africans. It had one of the largest slave markets and that building is still standing on 6 Chalmers Street. I heard about some slave rebellions in and around Charleston from some older Black men who hung outside of Gus' grocery store on the corner of Ashley Avenue and Fishburne Street near my house on Friday nights. The store was also a few yards from the old hanging tree on Ashley Avenue. I heard about the Stono Rebellion of September 9, 1739 with 35 whites and 50 Blacks killed. I learned that in 1822, Denmark Vesey, a self-educated Black man, who was also a carpenter, purchased his freedom with $1500 he won in the East Bay Street Lottery. He used $600 out of his win to purchase his freedom. Inspired by the successful Haitian slave revolt in the summer of 1791, led by Toussaint L'Ouverture, Vesey and his Lieutenants organized nine thousand African Americans for a slave revolt in Charleston to begin on July 14, 1822, but it failed because two slaves told their white masters about the plan. Therefore, Denmark Vesey and 34 Black men were publicly hung in the streets of Charleston. Soon after the killing of Denmark Vesey the city of Charleston built an Armory to protect its white citizens. That place is now called "The Citadel." If that revolt had succeeded, it would have been the largest slave revolt in American history. The statue of Denmark Vesey created by Ed Dwight can be found at the historic Hampton Park in Charleston, South Carolina.

I also learned that Fort Sumter, which is located in the Charleston's Harbor is the place where the Civil War began on April 12, 1861. The Civil War left the city of Charleston in ruins. After the Civil War some people called Charleston "a city of the dead." Many of its white residences were either killed or run out the city by the Union Army. Leaving behind thousands former slaves and some white missionaries. After the Civil War ended, some former slaves from Charleston came together on Hampton Park to dig up the mass grave of fallen Union Soldiers. They reburied them in individual graves. Word got out into the community as to what those free slave men had done. Then the community came out to support the men. They had a big parade on the streets of Charleston which ended up on Hampton Park. There was a sermon given by a former slave. They prayed, sang songs and had a big picnic. They then recognized Monday, May 1, 1865 as "Declaration Day," which later became Memorial Day. To learn more about the first Memorial Day, go online and read the David W. Blight article, The First Decoration Day/Newark Star Ledger.

It wasn't hard to get around Charleston. I even went into customers' homes. Some were beautiful and some were just terrible. That's when I realized that not all Black people were poor or all white people rich. The people I came across were nice to me. I worked from 3:30 to 7:30 p.m.

I worked for the drugstore for about a year. One Monday evening, I was on Cannon Street making a delivery. After dropping off a prescription I rode by George's Shoe Shop, owned by a Black man. To my knowledge, it was the only Black shoe shop in town. George knew my mother, my father and my grandparents. He asked me how he could help me. "I don't want anything," I said. "I just want to look at your shoes." He had lots of shoes in the window that were on sale.

"You see anything you like?" he asked me.

"Yes sir, the brown and beige half-boot." He took one from the pair in the window and told me to try it on. It felt good on my foot.

He said, "You can have it for $5.00."

"Can I put them on lay-away? I only have $2.00 now."

He nodded, "Okay, give me what you have." The following Saturday, after making a drugstore delivery, I stopped by the shoe shop to finish paying for my shoes. There were other people in the store. Some of the men were at a booth getting their shoes shined. When it was my time to be served, George handed me my new shoes. He said, "I see you riding that bike around here all the time. You got a job?"

"Yes, sir. I deliver prescriptions to customers' homes for the drug store on Rutledge Avenue."

Nodding in approval, George said, "I need a boy to deliver my shoes. How much are you getting paid?

"Fifteen dollars a week," I told him.

Smiling, "I'll give you seventeen."

"Okay, but I have to check with my mother." I went back to the drugstore and worked until it closed. The owner paid me for the week. When I got home I told my mother about the delivery job offer at the shoe shop. She left the decision to me. The job offered the same number of hours and just a little more money. I made my decision—take the job. Later, I told Eddie my plans and asked him if he would be interested in taking the drugstore job I was leaving. Sure enough he was.

The next Monday after school I went to the drugstore and picked up a prescription to deliver. Then I stopped by the shoe shop to tell Mr. George I would take the job he had offered. He told me to come to work as soon as possible. Then I stopped by the park and told my brother to meet me at the drugstore because I was quitting and I wanted the owner to meet him.

I went into the store and sat in a corner chair and waited for my brother to come. Then I took him with me to the back of the store where the owner was working. I told him I needed to talk to him.

I said, "Mr. Thomas, I have a job offer that is paying me more money. This will be my last week working here. This is my brother Eddie. Can you please give him my job?"

Mr. Thomas looked at me, then at Eddie. "Eddie, your brother is a good worker. I see you across the street playing basketball all the time. Are you ready to take your brother's place?"

Eddie answered, "Yes sir. I can do the job."

The owner asked, "What's your new job?" I told him. He shook my hand and congratulated me. He also thanked me for bringing in my brother.

I worked each Tuesday through Saturday. Saturday was my big tip-making day and the day I got my weekly pay check. There was now another Black boy named Spite working there. When I was not delivering shoes Spite would teach me how to shine shoes. He knew how to make the rag pop when he shined. All the men wanted him to shine their shoes. Spite would sing as he shined: "Hambone, hambone have you heard?" while the rag went, *pop- pop-pop.* "Papa gonna buy me a mocking bird." Normally I would shine shoes only after Mr. George had fixed them, but soon I learned Spite's technique and would help out when he was busy. The shoe shop was quite popular. I would hear all the gossip going on in town from the customers chatting with Mr. George.

I used to love standing outside and talking to the girls passing by. They would say, "How you doing, shoe shine boy?" I would respond, "Pretty girl, I'll make you mine if you'll stop and give me some time." If Mr. George saw me outside talking to a girl too long, he would come to the door, "Marvin, whose paying you, me or that girl?" Then I would hurry back inside. By now, I had developed a good relationship with him. He'd say, "Those girls are going to get you in trouble one day."

I delivered and shined shoes for about a year. Then, it was time to move on to more adventurous things.

CHAPTER 8

House of Pain

Meanwhile, I was still working at the shoe shop. By this time, a lot of changes were occurring in my house. My mother's sister, Aunt Loretta, had gotten stabbed to death in New York City by a woman she knew. My mother was deeply hurt. She traveled to New York to my other aunt's apartment to help her arrange the funeral.

Then, as soon as Mama returned to Charleston, she had to go right back to New York to bury her baby brother, William. He had also been stabbed to death in a fight. These were some sad times in our family.

My eldest sister, Miriam married Mack McMillian, and later they had a daughter, Faith. Clarissa was dating Troy, and his cousin Bobby was dating my sister, Annette. Years later, Annette and Bobby Carson got married. Mamie became pregnant and gave birth to our niece Yolanda on November 7, 1971. Little Yolanda brought a lot of love and joy into our family. She was everyone's baby. The whole community helped Mamie raise her. Little did we know in those early years how proud she would eventually make us. She became a high achiever, maintaining an "A" average from the first grade through high school and was Salutatorian of the class of 1989 at Burke

High School. She was the first grandchild to go to college and she graduated with honors.

Eddie continued to work at the drugstore for about six months in 1972. One night he came home, ate dinner, and came into the bedroom we shared with our little sister Izetta. I slept on the top of our bunk bed and Eddie slept on the bottom. Izetta slept on the summer bed across from the bunk bed. Izetta and I were watching a program on television. Eddie had a habit of doing what he wanted to do and decided to change the channel. I got up and changed it back. Eddie changed it again. When I stood up to change it back again, he punched me in the face and we started fighting. When I hit him in his jaw, he grabbed his face and seemed to be in a lot of pain. I wondered why since I hadn't hit him hard enough to hurt. When he started spitting out blood, I knew it was serious and told him I was sorry. He started crying. I thought I must have knocked out one of his teeth, but he said it wasn't his tooth that hurt. The bleeding eventually stopped. He didn't run to tell Mama on me since he knew he had started the fight.

The next morning as he was lying in the bed, I noticed that he was still holding his jaw. Obviously, his jaw was still hurting, and I was very much concerned. We were all getting up and dressing for school or work and Mama was cooking breakfast.

Eddie walked into the kitchen and told Mama that his mouth was hurting him really badly. Mama asked him if anything had happened to cause the pain. He still didn't tell her that I had hit him the night before but said his jaw was hurting when he woke up. She told him to sit down and open his mouth. The gums on the right side of his mouth were still bleeding. She knew that was the cause of his pain and said she would take him to the dentist as soon as everyone left the house.

When I got home from school, Mama told me that Eddie had been admitted to Medical College Hospital so that a doctor could examine his jaw. A few hours later, she got a call from the hospital saying that my parents should come right away. Mama stopped cooking and asked Clarissa to finish preparing the meat. She and Daddy caught a cab to the hospital.

My sisters and I were very quiet and the house felt lonely. We prayed for Eddie. I felt very guilty about my punch to his jaw. We sat a long time in silence.

Hours later, my parents came back home and, side by side, called my sisters and me into the living room. Mama was crying. When she was able to talk, she told us that Eddie had cancer. My sisters started to cry. I didn't know what cancer was, but I knew it had to be bad.

Mamie asked, "Is he going to live?" My mother told her that the doctors were going to perform surgery the following morning. It was one of the saddest days of my life.

My eldest brother "Wonnie" stopped by the house on his way home from work and Mama told him the news. He asked me what had happened to Eddie. "He's too young to have cancer," he said. I cried and told the family that Eddie had started a fight the night before and I had punched him in the face after he first punched me.

Wonnie said, "That wouldn't cause him to have cancer." I felt somewhat relieved but was still afraid. By now, everyone was crying, including Daddy. Wonnie was heavy into the ministry by now, and he had us join hands and form a circle as he prayed to God for Eddie and our family.

Early the next morning we all got up and went to the hospital to be with Eddie while he had surgery. We stayed at the hospital all day and half of the night. When we were allowed to see him, half of his jaw had been removed. His head and face were all wrapped up in gauze and he was still sedated. He would occasionally open his eyes a little and then close them again.

Eventually a white male doctor came into the waiting room to greet us. He was surprised that Eddie had so many sisters and brothers. The doctor was cheerful and told us that the surgery had gone fine but that Eddie would have to undergo chemotherapy for about six months to kill any remaining cancer cells. Nevertheless, for the next two years we spent countless hours in the hospital with Eddie. My mother just about lived there. Eddie had become her priority. Whenever he got a chance to come home we all celebrated. He had become the center of our attention, the main attraction. He had gone through so much with the surgery and chemotherapy, but my brother was one tough guy.

CHAPTER 9

Trouble On Bogard Street

When I was in seventh grade one of my classmates was a girl named Wanda Lawton. She was the cousin of our classmate Darcy Phatt. He and I became good friends. One day after school I invited him to my house. My mother asked who his parents were? My mother told me that Darcy's mother and she grew up together. And that Darcy could be my friend. This was the beginning of a life long friendship. Darcy knew how much I loved Wanda and took me over to her house after dinner. We walked from my house to her house. She lived on Rose Land near Bogard Street. I was not familiar with this neighborhood, but my interest in Wanda started me to visit Bogard Street regularly. Bogard Street was very different than any other street I had been on. All the businesses were owned and run by Black people. It was a street full of life and energy. It has Juke joints with pool tables. Women and men would be dancing in them to the latest songs of the 60's and 70's any night of the week. I saw men and boys shooting dice behind houses for money. I saw some bad fighting going on also. To those who were hungry there was a soul food restaurant cooking up great food you could smell in the air. When I told some of my buddies about Bogard Street, they started to spend time there too. We made a lot of new friends there and had interesting conversations with them about life. There were also a lot of pretty girls. It wasn't long before my friends and I felt like this was where we were welcome and belonged.

I was impressed with the way many of the men on the street dressed. They wore red, purple, yellow, and light blue two-piece suits with matching shoes. During the winter they also wore fine hats; some of them even wore leather jackets or mink coats. I really dug the cool walk some of the older men displayed. I wanted to dress like them and learn to walk that cool walk they had mastered. They became my role models.

On Valentine's Day I gave Wanda a red bubble gum ring with a stone in it. When I told her how much I loved her, she kissed me and held me tight. I saw stars! I continued to visit her all through the summer. Then our love for one another faded away although we remained friends. She and Spencer began talking and fell in love. Years later they had a son, Jamal.

By the time we got to high school, my brother Eddie's health had improved and his cancer was now in remission. During the summer, Eddie, our friends and I started getting into trouble. Gus, a Greek, owned a grocery store a few houses from ours. He caught Eddie stealing some butter cookies and chased him down the street with a broom. Our friend, whom we called Buttercup, saw the chase; he laughed so hard that he nicknamed Eddie Gus. The owner of the store told our mother what Eddie did and he barred him from coming into his store.

We loved hanging on Bogard Street. Most of the children were our classmates, like Larry Polite. He and I were classmates and good friends. He was short and very competitive in everything he did. When I invited Larry to my house my mother knew who he was. His mother and mine were childhood friends. They both were pregnant with us at the same time. I was born in April and Larry was born in August 1959. He became a part of my new circle of friends. Larry is still one of my best friends. Eddie, Larry and Anthony Bradley were always at Michelle Park playing sports. Anthony Bradley was in my class also. He was a very smart student. He and Eddie hung out together a lot. I was never good at playing sports. I was more into dating girls and learned how to play cards and shoot pool.

If my mother had known about the things my brother and I did on Bogard Street, she would have stopped us from going there. I saw men get cut and beaten on Bogard Street; so I learned how to defend myself. My friend Fishmouth, who was only a year older than me, would usually be the one to start a fight with one of the street boys. When he and I got into a fight I would bite down on my tongue for strength. After the playful fight he named me "Bite." Sometimes Spencer and Fishmouth would wrestle in the street. Fishmouth nicknamed Spencer Black Ace. We called him Ace. Ace has been like a brother to me over fifty years. Even though we fought with Fishmouth, we would never really try to hurt one another. Fishmouth simply needed to know that we knew how to fight in case we ever really had to. After all, there were other gangs than ours in the city.

Fishmouth knew all of the bootleggers on Bogard Street and persuaded Nut, Ace, Eddie, and me to drink wine and sometimes stronger alcohol. By this time, Spencer's brother, Bunny had stopped hanging out with us. He preferred to stay at home. After collecting money from us he'd go and buy the bottles and bring them back to us. Most of the time, we drank cheap Wild Irish Rose wine. I loved Fishmouth's bravery; however, he didn't give a damn about anyone but himself. Whatever he wanted he got. Also, he either liked you or hated you. I only saw one white boy walking down Bogard Street. Fishmouth asked him where he was going. He told him that he was just going walking. Fishmouth beat him up for being in the wrong community. One thing he loved was music, especially the music of Barry White. He could not sing, but we nicknamed him Barry White. Fishmouth had one problem. He could not attract the girls. I don't remember that he ever had a girlfriend. It could be that he had neither love or had no patience for girls. As for the rest of us, the girls were crazy about us.

Bogard Street and its activities made up our world. On many a Saturday night we'd stay up all night after returning from a party. Our hang out spot was on the steps of Ms. Hamp's house, an elderly Black lady. It was across the street from Porters Court near Sires Street. We would sometimes sit in front of her house from sunrise to sunset planning what we were going to do next. We'd ride our bikes into the white section of town around 4 a.m. on Sunday morning. We would hide in the bushes and wait until the newspaper truck delivered the Sunday newspapers. After the truck left, we would gather up the bundles of papers and flee. We'd hop on our bikes and ride about ten deep—two boys to a bike. Whoever rode on the handlebars would tightly hold on to the newspapers while the other boys paddle as fast as he could back to Bogard Street. We would sleep for about two hours at one of our houses and then by 7 a.m. we would be fully dressed and stationed on some of the busiest street corners in Charleston to sell the pilfered newspapers. We had cleared twenty dollars or more by 9 a.m. Satisfied, we would return to our homes to rest. When my mother asked us where we got the money, Eddie and I lied; we told her we had a paper route. We used our money to buy the latest fashions at Father & Sons Men's Store on King Street. With our new 'business,' we kept clothes on lay-away. It was the only store that sold the extreme fads and loud colors that we so admired. We thought we looked good in them. The Jewish owner made a lot of money from us.

The first time I ever broke into a grocery store, I was assisting Fishmouth and some of the other gang members. By now, we were smoking a lot of weed and drinking wine. I didn't know why Fishmouth decided to break into that Black man's store. The store was one of our favorite places to shop. Whatever we needed, the owner would have given us— on credit, if need be.

There were times I was afraid of Fishmouth. He was sometimes high on some really heavy drugs—cocaine or anything he could get his hands on. That night he asked me to crawl into the store through the opening he had created using a crowbar. I was afraid but did it anyhow. Once I had crawled in, I ran to the back door of the store to let Fishmouth and the rest of the gang in. We stole all kinds of meat and stocked up on cookies, potato chips, and candy. We were never caught breaking into that store, but I promised myself not to let anyone ever again push me into doing something like that.

◆ ◆ ◆

When I was in the tenth grade at Burke High School on the west side of town, I met a tenth-grade cheerleader who attended C.A. Brown High School on the east side. Every day just after noon, the school bus brought her to Burke to participate in a home economics class. One of her friends introduced us one day and we exchanged phone numbers. Her name was Jhiquitta. She called me around 9:00 that night. We talked about everything that was happening in our lives. Our nightly conversations went on for weeks. Once we agreed to become a couple Jhiquitta demanded so much of my attention that my friends on Bogard Street began teasing me about being in love with her.

My Jhiquitta had pretty legs. She loved kissing me after school outside of the school gate. She wanted the girls at my school to know that I was her man. On many occasions, Jhiquitta and I wanted to have sex. However, she never wanted to skip school to go with me to my friend's house. Both of us were a part of a large family, so making love at one of our homes was totally out of the question. Because I rarely had money, it never dawned on me to take her to a motel.

One Tuesday night in October 1975, I was visiting Jhiquitta when I noticed a group of Black boys heading toward her house. I recognized them as the Jackson Street Panthers, a gang of notorious fighters. As I watched them getting closer, I asked her to let me go inside her house until they passed. A while back I had heard from my brother Eddie that Mark, a member of the Panthers gang, did not like me. I quickly slipped into her house with Jhiquitta following me. It turned out that Mark liked Jhiquitta and wanted her for himself.

One of the gang members was Jhiquitta's brother. He came into the house and saw us sitting on the couch together. We exchanged greetings. He cautioned me to be careful with his sister and then went back outside to join the gang as they continued walking down the street.

When they were finally out of sight, I got on my new 10-speed bicycle, kissed her goodnight, and rode over to the west side of town where I felt safe. Later that night I called Jhiquitta and told her what I had heard from my brother Eddie. I told her that if she wanted to continue to see me, she would have to come to my side of town. Jhiquitta continued to be my girlfriend, but she was tired of my refusal to visit her at home because I had too many enemies on the east side and didn't want to put my life in danger and become a statistic. Too many young Black men were being beaten and killed on the east side of town. A month later we ended the relationship but remained good friends while we were in school.

By the time I was in eleventh grade, I had become more and more involved with drugs. My first encounter was with marijuana and a pill called Strawberry Mess. Once I took Strawberry Mess with some syrup just before going with three of my friends to a Sunday night concert to see Jimmy Lancaster. The music sounded loud and freaky. When the concert was over, I was so high that it was impossible for me to walk home; I had to catch a cab. I don't remember which one of us boys paid the cab driver. We went into the house. Ace, who often spent the night at our house was like family, Eddie and I went upstairs to the boys' room. My mother and father were in their room sleeping. I was talking out of my head. My older sister Miriam, who happened to be spending the night came into our room and saw how high I was. Eddie told her I was high on drugs. Somehow, she got me moved into the girls' room where my sisters sat up all night trying to get me sober and relaxed. They took turns rubbing my back, feeding me, and putting ice on my head. It's a good thing our parents never woke up! I promised myself that I would never take Strawberry Mess again.

CHAPTER 10

Slow Learner

In September 1973, I was socially promoted from Mitchell Elementary School to Burke High School. I was thirteen years old and in the eighth grade. Like my classmates, I wore my best clothes on the first day of school. I don't remember seeing any white students, although by then the schools had been integrated. Mr. Taylor, a brown skinned, baldheaded man with glasses, was my homeroom teacher; he also taught business courses. Larry Polite, Darcy Pratt, and Slede Green, my best friends, were in the same homeroom along with several of the kids I knew from Simonton and Rhett Elementary schools. Mr. Taylor had taught my older sisters how to type. He welcomed all the students to Burke High School and told us that we would get out of school what we put into it and we should all do our best to make good grades. Then he gave each student a class schedule. When I looked at mine, I was surprised. I had no idea that I would be going to so many different classes with new teachers and students.

The class I hated most was English. The teacher, whom I will call Ms. Morgan, was terribly strict and rarely smiled. She didn't allow students to hang around outside her classroom after the bell rang.

On the second day of class, Ms. Morgan called on me to read the first paragraph of our English textbook. I was embarrassed as I attempted to read. I could recognize only a few words without her help. The students in the back of the room started snickering. I was so terribly humiliated that I wanted to die. After I got through struggling through the paragraph and the laughter ceased somewhat, Ms. Morgan told me to see her after class. The girl behind me read the next paragraph without any difficulty, and no one laughed at her. I bowed my head and cried silently, trying to hide my tears.

After class was over, Ms. Morgan tried to console me. She told me not to feel bad but to realize that I had to work harder at learning. She advised me not to hang around bad boys and to concentrate on my education. My problem was that I had no educational foundation upon which to build. I should never have been admitted to high school because I was not prepared. In spite of my mother's protests, I was sent to high school anyhow. I was never really sure what I was supposed to do with my books when I went home after school. I was ashamed to ask anybody for help with my learning difficulties. My sister, Annette would help me occasionally when she was not tired from her job. My mother had stopped whooping me by then. She must have realized that I was doing the best I could and whoopings wouldn't make me smarter.

After a few days, Ms. Morgan had me transferred to the Special Education class where she felt I could receive more help. It was in those classes that I began to improve in my studies. The teachers were more patient with me. By the time I got to eleventh grade I could at least read a little better. I was reading books like *The Cat in the Hat* and *The Lady and the Tramp*. I stayed in the Special Education program through the twelfth grade. I was still not sure I could function in a normal classroom because I didn't know how to write an essay. I had never understood mathematics except multiplication. Eventually I took a class in brick masonry, but I wasn't even good at that. I felt like a complete failure.

CHAPTER 11

Our New Home

Finally, after years of being irresponsible, my father settled down enough to buy our own house. My sister Miriam had heard about a program sponsored by the city of Charleston for first time homeowners. She contacted the city and got all the information for my parents. Charleston was building new townhouses on Grove Street. Clarissa co-signed the application with my father, who was working on the city garbage truck picking up trash and was supporting the family. The application was approved to buy the house at 30 Grove Street. My mother was very happy and so were all the children.

On a Monday night we moved into the white two-story townhouse trimmed in green. It was in a gated house. The house had three bedrooms and a bath on the second floor and another bathroom on the first floor. My parents slept in the master bedroom. My four sisters, who were still living at home, Clarissa, Annette, Izetta, Mamie, and her daughter Yolanda, slept in one room, which had a bunk bed and a single bed. Eddie and I shared a room that had one bunk bed.

Two weeks after we moved into our new home, my mother had a housewarming on a Sunday after church. My great-grandmother, Mamie J. Simmons, and my grandmother, Eva Rivers, came as well as many other relatives and friends who brought various household gifts. My older sisters, who were all working, contributed furniture.

My mother had spent all day Saturday shopping and cooking for the Sunday feast. In our dining room was a long table with all of Mama's favorite dishes. Both the minister from my great-grandfather's church and our minister brother Wonnie offered prayers of blessing on our new home. All of us were especially happy that day.

My sisters started a tradition of having parties on Saturday nights. We provided music with a disco light record player. Our living room became the Soul Train dance floor. The music was very loud, but the neighbors never complained. We had a bar and enough stools to accommodate our guests. Free alcoholic drinks were provided for anyone who wanted to partake, but the dinners my mother prepared were for sale. My brother Clifford, his wife Barbara, and their son Slugger usually came from up north. Two of my cousins Elaine and Porgy were present as well as many of our friends. My brother Wonnie was there, too. He didn't drink but he never judged those who did. He enjoyed listening to the music. His favorite artists were Sam Cooke, Jackie Wilson, and Chubby Checker. He weighed over 200 pounds and had a big appetite. When Mama made his plate, he always requested "a heavy load."

As word got around, the number of people continued to increase. There was usually wall- to-wall people. Everybody seemed to be having a good time dancing, joking, eating, drinking, or just listening to the music. In good weather, some of the people went outside where it was quieter and they could carry on conversations.

Daddy often came home late and drunk, parking his bicycle in the front yard. After greeting the people outside, he would come in and join the dancers. He had a special way of dancing that everyone seemed to enjoy. He would throw both hands in the air, moving all of his fingers, and shuffling his feet in rhythm in a special way that was uniquely his own. Other dancers would stop to watch him do his silly dance moves.

After a while, my mother would say, "Come on now, you done entertained enough. It's time for you to go to your room." He always resisted but my little nephew Slugger and niece Yolanda would help my mother push him up the stairs. It would be past midnight when the last guests left. Each of us children had an assigned duty to perform during and after the party when it was time to clean up.

Through our parties my family gained a lot of friends, both Black and white. Wayne, a white guy who worked with Clarissa, was like a family member. We didn't see color in him or any of the other white guests. All we felt was love.

On Sunday morning, Mama and my sisters counted the money from the dinners. It helped to pay a lot of bills. The family was together and close, and I remember this period as one of the happiest in my life. The other children and my parents were happy, too.

Those Saturday parties went on for years, and I thought they would never end. I thought we would be happy together forever. But one sister after another got married and we all grew up and moved out of our parents' home, but memories of 30 Grove Street will always be especially happy.

CHAPTER 12

St. Francis Marion Hotel

When I was sixteen years old, I went job-hunting after school on King Street in the downtown business district of Charleston. It was a fall day in 1975. I was still working part-time for the *News Inquirer* stuffing papers at night. It was just a temporary job. No one cared if you came to work or not. As I approached the St. Francis Marion Hotel, I saw someone who looked familiar standing in front. I recognized his face but not his name. He was wearing an Afro and was well dressed in a yellow jacket and a clean white shirt with a Black tie. His Black shoes looked freshly polished. As I approached him, I remembered that his name was Aubrey, a high school senior and stopped to talk to him. I was still in the tenth grade. He said that he planned to enlist in the Army after graduation. I told him I was looking for a job and asked if he knew of anything available. "As a matter of fact, I do," he said. "My bell captain is looking for someone to work the evening shift with him."

"Great!" I said. "I'd like to apply." He told me to follow him into the hotel.

We went up some stairs into the lobby. To the right was a small room that he said was the bell captain's office. "Wait here," he said while he went inside. When he closed the door, I discovered that it had both an upper and lower opening. After a few minutes, he opened the top door and handed me an application to fill out. He directed me to a seat in the lobby where I could fill it out. I completed it and gave it back to him and he promised to give it to his bell captain when he got in.

After waiting a few minutes, a short, light-complexion Black man came downstairs. I couldn't help noticing his large belly. Aubrey introduced us, "This is Mr. Mose Smalls, the bell captain; this is Marvin Alston, a buddy of mine from school. He's interested in the bellhop's job and just filled out an application."

Mr. Smalls smiled at me, "I know who you are. Didn't you work at George's shoe shop across the street from my house on Cannon Street?"

"Yes, sir."

"I think I know your grandparents, too. Aren't they Eva Rivers and Mamie Simmons?" I nodded.

"Good people," he said. "When can you start working?"

"Any time," I answered.

"Okay, come back tomorrow evening at 4:30. Aubrey will be here to train you." I thanked both and shook hands, then walked down the stairs into the street feeling happy about my new job. I took the Meeting Street bus back home to tell my family the good news. As always, they were very happy for me.

After school the next day, I went home, enjoyed dinner, and then caught the Meeting Street bus getting off at Calhoun Street. I walked across

Calhoun Park to the St. Francis Marion Hotel where Aubrey was waiting for me. I greeted him with a soul brother handshake.

I followed him upstairs to the employees' laundry room to get my uniform. In the laundry room he introduced me to several Black middle-aged ladies who seemed very friendly. One of them asked my sizes—pants, jacket and shirt. My shoes were already well polished. After receiving my uniform, I followed Aubrey to the locker room where I could change my clothes. He told me to pick any one of the vacant lockers and reminded me to buy a lock as soon as possible. "When you finish dressing, meet me in the lobby." he said.

After I put on my new uniform, I looked at myself in the full-length mirror and thought I looked as sharp as Aubrey. Then I went downstairs and met him in front of the bell captain's office. He took me over to the registration desk and introduced me to the white clerks and switchboard operator who seemed pleased to meet me. Then we went down another flight of stairs to the restaurant where he introduced me to two very attractive Black waitresses. They jokingly advised me not to let Aubrey get me into trouble. From there we went back upstairs to the closed door to the bell captain's office. Aubrey said, "Mr. Smalls won't be here until five o'clock, and he sits inside the office, but the bellhops have to stand outside the office to be available to wait on customers."

In a few minutes, a bell rang and I followed Aubrey to the front desk where a white man with two bags had just arrived. Aubrey grabbed one bag and told me to pick up the other one. Together we led the guest to the elevator and pressed the button to the ninth floor. Then we all got off and escorted the guest to his room. Aubrey unlocked the door and we went inside where we set the luggage on special racks. Aubrey picked up a small white bucket and told the guest he'd be right back with some ice. I followed

Aubrey to the corner of the hallway where the ice machine was. After filling the bucket with ice, we returned to the man's door and Aubrey knocked. The guest opened the door, took the ice bucket and gave Aubrey a two-dollar tip. Aubrey thanked him and we left. As we approached the elevator, Aubrey gave me one of the dollar bills. He assured me, "You'll be leaving every night with some money in your pocket." At that moment I knew I was going to like my job.

When Mr. Smalls arrived that evening, he seemed glad to see me. He told me to call him Mose. "Is Aubrey doing a good job of training you, or should I fire him?" We both laughed. I told him that Aubrey was doing just fine. Mose settled himself in his office. As Aubrey was leaving the building to go home, Mose began telling me about the St. Francis Marion Hotel. He said the historic hotel was built in 1920 and that he was the first to be hired as a bell captain in 1924 when the hotel opened. He said the hotel was named after a white Revolutionary War hero, Francis Marion, who was also recognized as "The Swamp Fox." He told me that the hotel was known for its historic and famous clientele, adding that there was a good possibility I might meet some of these celebrities.

Then he shared some interesting and surprising information. He told me that he was the great-grandson of a famous Black man, Congressman Robert Smalls, who along with seven enslaved crewmen, courageously confiscated an armed Confederate transport ship, the C.S.S. Planter, from the heavily guarded Charleston Harbor and turned it over to the Union Army.

This happened on May 13, 1862 at three o'clock in the morning just before the beginning of the Civil War. Before attempting this dangerous action, his great-grandfather and his crewmen, Mose was told, prayed this prayer: "Oh Lord, we entrust ourselves into Thy hands. Like Thou didst for the Israelites in Egypt, please stand over us to our promised land of freedom." This bold move earned Robert Smalls a personal invitation to the White House by President Abraham Lincoln. After the Civil War, Robert Smalls went on to win five terms in Congress as a State Representative from South Carolina.

Edwin Smalls, owner of the famous Smalls Paradise Night Club in Harlem, was Mose's uncle. Smalls Paradise was famous for its big band orchestras, which were directed by such notables as Charlie Johnson, Duke Ellington, and Willie 'The Lion' Smith. The club was also famous during the 1920s for its waiters who entertained the clients by dancing the popular Charleston. "When my wife and I visited Smalls Paradise," Mose said, "we partied with Harlem Renaissance poets and writers like Langston Hughes, Alain Locke, Zora Neale Hurston, and Countee Cullen." Mose kept me in awe of Black history during the two and a half years that I worked with him at the St Francis Marion Hotel. I learned more history from him than I could have ever found in books.

Some nights after work, I'd walk alone down King Street and cross over to Meeting Street to buy fried chicken from the new Church's Fried Chicken fast food restaurant that my mother loved. I'd order a two-piece for her with some fried okra and a two-piece for me with French fries and a large strawberry soda that we'd share. I'd usually catch a cab home from Church's. My mother always sat near her bedroom window at night until all her children were in the house. I enjoyed these small meals at night in the dining room, eating and talking with my mother; this was our little ritual. Once we finished eating, I shared with Mama the tips that I had made that day, telling her to buy herself something nice. She was a full-time housewife, so my tips always put a smile on her face.

My brother Eddie got a job as a busboy at the Hyatt Hotel on Meeting Street about a mile away from where I worked. Mama said he never offered to share his tips with her as I did; he gave her only what she asked for. In our many talks, I told Mose that I had made plans to go to Atlantic City, New Jersey the following summer in 1976. He told me that if I did a good job until that time, I could go and he would hold my job until I came back. He had some older bellmen who had retired, but if he needed them, they would come and help out. I loved my job as a bellboy. I loved Mose's satisfaction with my work. True to his word, he allowed me to take off for the summer of 1976 to travel to Atlantic City and visit my older brother Clifford and his family.

Over the two years that I worked at the Francis Marion Hotel, I actually met some famous people: South Carolina Senator Strom Thurmond and Alabama Governor George Wallace who was then in a wheelchair. I also met the band members of Earth Wind and Fire and The Emotions, just to name a few. My days at the Francis Marion Hotel were especially rewarding and memorable.

CHAPTER 13

Summer Vacation

After my promotion to the twelfth grade my brother Clifford invited Eddie and me to an extended summer visit in Atlantic City, New Jersey with him, his wife, Barbara and their son, nicknamed "Slugger." We would get a chance to visit other relatives who lived nearby. On the morning of June 2, 1976, Wonnie arrived and after emotional goodbyes to our sisters, drove us to the Charleston airport. Mama sat in the front seat. I could sense that our leaving was affecting her; this would be our first time away from home. When we arrived at the airport and retrieved our luggage from the trunk, Mama kissed us with tears in her eyes, "Be good and have fun."

We arrived at Philadelphia International Airport excited about our first experience on an airplane. Clifford, with his hair braided, met us in the baggage claim area. He seemed as happy to see us as we were to see him. Once outside the airport, we looked with awe at all the streets and buildings in Philadelphia. Everything in this big northern city looked so different from Charleston! As we rode the sixty miles to Atlantic City, Clifford explained to us what he expected of us during our summer vacation, including getting jobs and buying our school clothes for the fall. "Don't get carried away by these fast-northern girls," he advised. "A lot of them are willing to have sex with a man the first time they meet them. Be sure to keep some condoms handy. I have a good supply; you won't even have to buy any. We don't want you to leave any babies behind." Eddie and I laughed, but he was serious.

We arrived at his house about three o'clock. Collecting our luggage, we followed Clifford through the alley to 730 Pearl Place, a modern brick two-story house, entering through the back door that led to the kitchen. Immediately, we smelled some good homemade food cooking, including spaghetti with Italian bread, one of my favorite dishes. Barbara entered the kitchen from the living room, a bright welcoming smile on her face. We hugged and kissed her. Her hair was braided, too; she was obviously pregnant. Before we could even ask, she said, "Any day now." Just then Slugger ran into the kitchen and we took turns picking him up and telling him how much he had grown since we last saw him. As soon as I put him down, he took my hand and dragged me to the front porch to introduce me to his dog, a large German shepherd named Duke, who was barking and wagging his tale furiously. I was scared out of my wits. When he stood up, he was taller than I was. I didn't want anything to do with him and quickly left the porch to go back to the living room couch. Everybody laughed at me. "He won't bite you," Slugger assured me. "He has teeth, doesn't he?" Slugger nodded. "Well, you keep that beast on the porch," I yelled.

Later that evening, Barbara's four sisters came to meet us and share the dinner Barbara had prepared. They all greeted us warmly in their unique New Jersey accent. Immediately, I liked all of them. All summer long we enjoyed their company. Ethelene, who lived across the street, was more like a real sister than an in-law. She was someone I could talk to about anything and get her advice. Pat was full of jokes and loved to cook for us. Debbie, who was my age, would share a lot of interesting conversations with me, and the youngest Freda was like a baby sister that I wanted to spoil.

After our first week there, I was awakened during the night by Clifford and Barbara's voices. I got out of bed and went downstairs to see if everything was okay. "Barbara's in labor," Clifford said. "We need to leave for the hospital right away."

"Do you want me to go with you?"

"No," he said. "We'll be okay. Go back to bed."

When I woke up some hours later to the aroma of the sausage and eggs Clifford was cooking. I went downstairs where Slugger and Eddie were already watching the news. It was Wednesday, June 9, 1976. I joined Clifford in the kitchen; he had a big grin on his face. "Congratulate me," he said. "I'm the father of a new baby girl. We named her Mahogany. Mother and baby are doing fine."

I gave him a big hug. "Congratulations, Daddy," I said.

After breakfast we all went to the hospital. Barbara was lying in bed with her new baby in her arms. Her face glowed with a look of joy and adoration. Eddie was the first one who asked to hold the baby. "Okay, but be sure to support her head," Barbara cautioned, "And don't breathe any of your germs on her."

When it was my turn, I whispered, "Welcome to the world, little one. Have a good life." Barbara brought Mahogany home two days later to the room that had already been turned into a nursery and was back to cooking as usual.

After two weeks in Atlantic City, neither Eddie nor I had found jobs on the boardwalk. Then we thought we had found something. Barbara's sister, Ethelene and their mother both worked at the local hospital, but the workers were presently on strike. To make extra money they picked blueberries on a farm. They suggested that we go with them until we could find something better. A day or so later, Eddie and I ate an early breakfast, packed brown bag lunches and joined them for the long drive to the farm. When we arrived, several Mexican families were already at work with more arriving. "Watch out for snakes," Ethelene warned us as we got out of her mother's car. After checking in with a white man who gave us instructions and seemed to be in charge, we started working. The sun was much hotter than I had expected; I must have taken fifty water breaks in addition to stopping for a quick lunch. By the end of the eight-hour day, I had picked two large crates of blueberries and was feeling proud of myself. I just knew I had made a lot of money. To my surprise, after my crates were weighed, the man gave me only two dollars, about the same amount that he gave Eddie. The Mexicans must have worked much harder and made much more money than we did. On the ride back to the city, I told Ethelene I would never work on anyone's farm again. "Same here," Eddie snapped.

Ethelene told us where we could get identification cards with our pictures on them. They would help us get better jobs, she said. The next day Eddie and I went downtown to Atlantic Avenue to get ID cards, giving our ages falsely as eighteen. Then we went to every hotel on the boardwalk and filled out applications. Eddie got hired before I did. Soon after, I got a job in the housekeeping department of Hotel Dennis. I would be working Monday through Friday from 8:00 a.m. to 4:30 p.m. and would receive a free lunch.

I loved my job on the very first day. I met and mingled with interesting people from all over the country. I especially liked those from Philadelphia and New York. Some of the men I saw in the lobby were well-dressed African Americans who were usually in the company of pretty white and Black girls. I was told by several of the room service workers that they also had a lot of money, suggesting that they were pimps. I eventually got to know a very attractive, shapely, brown-skin maid in her twenties who seemed to take a liking to me. Most of our conversation was flirtatious. One day she gave me her address and invited me to her apartment after work. I anticipated having sex with her and wondered how it would be. But I forgot about my date and instead went to a bar with some of my male coworkers where we drank Wild Irish Rose and played pool. We consumed about six bottles. When we left, I was so drunk I could barely stand up. When I got home, my condition was obvious. Clifford told me I was making a fool of myself and chastised me, saying I was going to be a drunk just like Daddy. "I ought to send you back home to Charleston. You're a disgrace." I had no appetite and stumbled upstairs to my room to sleep it off.

The next morning, I woke up at five o'clock and headed downstairs to find something to eat. On the landing I noticed a bookcase filled with books. Eddie had already started reading *The Autobiography of Malcolm* X. Maybe if Clifford saw me reading he would forget about my being drunk the night before. Glancing over the titles, I saw a book called *Nigger* by Dick Gregory. After eating a few bites, I picked up the book; I sat down and opened it to the first page. I found the book easy to read and understand; it was very interesting and sometimes humorous. The author had a great deal to say about the Klu Klux Klan and white supremacists. When Clifford came downstairs later and saw me reading, he seemed pleased. "Now that's the thing to do. You need to be reading more instead of drinking." He joined me on the living room couch. I apologized about coming home drunk. He accepted my apology but reminded me not to become an alcoholic like Daddy. He began telling me more about Dick Gregory. The more I learned, the more I wanted to know. Remembering my reading problem, he said, "I've got a plan. Try to read one chapter every day. Then after breakfast, tell the family what you learned from the chapter you read the day before. While you're reading, make a note of at least one word you didn't understand

and had to look up, and give the definition. That way, you'll increase your vocabulary."

When I came home from work later that day, I sat down and watched the news on TV, something I had never done before. When the news reporter used the word *optimistic*, I asked Clifford what it meant. "Look it up in the dictionary," he said. He helped me find it and understand the definition. The next morning, I surprised Clifford by using *optimistic* in a sentence. He was very pleased and I was very happy. I realized that, if I put my mind to it, I could learn to read and understand more difficult words than those in the reading material I was used to. I felt that my world was beginning to change. That summer I read five more books.

Early on Saturday and Sunday mornings Clifford, Eddie, Slugger and I would use the bicycles on the porch to ride to the boardwalk. On the beach, we saw men swimming, shapely girls in bikinis swimming or walking in the white sand near the water and others investigating the endless shops that sold clothing, jewelry, souvenirs, and other items. The most interesting part of the boardwalk was the three piers that extended over the ocean. All of the piers were amusement parks where we saw families enjoying themselves. Riding along the boardwalk, we would often talk, and I felt a great bonding with my brothers and nephew. I remember Clifford saying, "You know what it takes to be a man? A real man takes care of his wife and children. A real man reads books and continues to learn and educate himself."

Occasionally Barbara and the baby would join us, enjoying a seafood dinner at a restaurant or taking in a movie. On some Saturday nights we would dress up and Clifford would take Barbara, Eddie and me to a nightclub where we would dance or to the Cotton Club in the Black district on Kentucky Avenue. (This club is not to be confused with the original Cotton Club in Harlem.) At these nightclubs I developed a taste for Long

Island iced tea, Vodka and cranberry juice, and cognac straight. Clifford made sure I didn't drink enough alcohol to get drunk.

I don't recall ever going to church on Sunday mornings. Instead, we just took it easy and enjoyed our day off. In the evening after dinner, we would turn on the TV to watch the news and "Sixty Minutes." Clifford felt the importance of knowing what was going on around the world. If I didn't understand some of what I heard, he or Barbara would explain it to me—a means of informal education. Once after the news broadcast, we watched the 1976 Olympics and cheered as Carl Lewis won four gold medals.

Eddie read a lot of books and worked puzzles in the newspapers. He and Barbara, who was a teacher, enjoyed talking. I often asked questions and learned a great deal from their discussions. One of their favorite TV shows was "Wheel of Fortune." I was amazed every time one of them came up with the right answer.

In spite of my initial fear of Slugger's dog, I eventually got up the courage to go walking with them. It was a way of bonding with my nephew. He was about seven years old and enjoyed football. Eddie and I would take turns throwing a football back and forth with him. We even got into the habit of running around the block with him to prepare him for playing in the community pee-wee team.

One Saturday Clifford and Barbara took us to New York City by Greyhound bus to visit Uncle Felix and Aunt Grace. They lived in an apartment on Riverside Drive. Aunt Grace was my godmother; she was the person who named me Marvin. When we came out of the Holland Tunnel, it was like entering an entirely new world. Many of the buildings were so tall that I couldn't even see their tops. All the pedestrians seemed to be in a hurry and I had never seen so many taxi cabs in my life. Eddie and I were completely in awe. It was our first time in Manhattan. Uncle Felix was waiting for us outside the Greyhound Station. After warm greetings, we all piled into his car and headed for his apartment. Once there, we were greeted by our cousins, Jamie and Nikki, who had breakfast waiting. Aunt Grace seemed to know how anxious we were to go sightseeing. When we finished breakfast, she kissed Eddie and me and gave us some spending money.

Then we followed Clifford, Barbara holding the baby, and Slugger to the elevator and to the street where we took the subway downtown to the World Trade Center. We went into the building and took an elevator to the top floor. When we stepped out of the elevator the sight was beautiful and scary to me. I had never been so high up in a building. You could look out the big tall glass windows and you could see the 5 boroughs of New York City and beyond. You could look down and see people walking around looking like ants. We exited the World Trade Center and continued walking until we got to a restaurant on Broadway near Times Square later that evening. After we were seated, we ordered drinks. Being with my older brother made me feel grown up enough to order a drink I had never had before—a Manhattan straight. The others ordered soft drinks. It was too early for lunch, so after we finished our drinks we went sightseeing until late in the evening. As I was looking out the window in the restaurant I remembered Mose telling me that there was a lot to see in New York, but I never knew there was so much. I couldn't believe that I was actually seeing places that I had only heard of before.

When we got back to Uncle Felix's apartment, Eddie and I were so excited that we weren't a bit tired. After grabbing a bite to eat, we decided to go back out, this time just the two of us. Clifford gave us directions for catching the subway to Harlem, making sure we had Uncle Felix's phone number in case we got lost. We got off at Lenox Avenue and 125th Street, remembering that this was the neighborhood where Malcolm X used to hang out. The first thing we saw when we got off the train was two Black women fighting on the sidewalk. My first instinct was to try to separate them, but Eddie stopped me, telling me how dangerous it would be to get involved. We noticed that the people we saw in Harlem were different from those downtown in the Times Square and 42nd Street area.

Walking down Lenox Avenue, we heard a lot of noise coming from one of the open windows of an apartment building. We decided to investigate. We found the door where the noise was coming from open. An older Black man invited us to come in and have a drink. A lot of older African Americans were dancing or playing cards. No one seemed to care that they didn't know us; we just blended in. After drinking two beers, we left the party and boarded the train. As soon as we got off the subway at 42nd Street, we were approached by two Puerto Rican boys who were selling marijuana. We were curious and ended up buying four joints at two dollars each. We watched other people smoking and lit up ourselves. We began feeling high as we continued our sightseeing. Every few yards we saw young ladies of all ethnic backgrounds selling something or soliciting money in exchange for sex. We had never seen so many X-rated movie theaters as we did on 42nd Street. We found the area so interesting that we lost track of time. Before we knew it, it was 4 o'clock in the morning.

When we got back to Uncle Felix's, he didn't mention the time but asked if we had enjoyed ourselves. We certainly had. In fact, we had such a good time that, after a few hours' sleep, we went back downtown, this time with Clifford and Barbara who wanted to make sure we saw such sights as the United Nations building. Later, Uncle Felix drove us to the Bronx for a quick visit with our mother's sister, Aunt Roana, and her son Michael. Then we went back to say goodbye to Aunt Grace, Jamie and Nikki. As we rode the bus again I admired the tall skyscrapers. I knew that I would come back to New York City some day and that I wanted to spend my adult life in the North.

On the way back to Atlantic City, I realized that we had only one more week before our vacation would end and we would head back home to Charleston. After we got back to Clifford's house he and Slugger took Eddie and me to a couple of department stores on Atlantic Avenue where we bought back-to-school clothes.

On our last day, Clifford drove Barbara and the baby, Slugger, Eddie and me to Philadelphia to visit Aunt Alice, our father's baby sister, and her grown children. Aunt Alice showed us an album of family photos and bought us some refreshments to take with us on the plane. We really wanted to stay longer, but it was getting time to catch our flight. I felt very sad leaving after the good times we had enjoyed. Our summer had also been an educational experience for me. I learned more that summer than in eleven years of school. Still, I realized that I had a lot more to learn. We thanked Clifford and Barbara for a wonderful vacation; we could tell that they had enjoyed our visit too. We hugged and said our emotional goodbyes as we prepared to board the plane for home.

CHAPTER 14

The Bellhop Pimp

Back to Charleston. Mr. Mose Smalls, my supervisor at the St. Francis Marion Hotel, welcomed me back to my evening job as a bellboy. My co-worker Aubrey had quit his job at the hotel to join the Army. I was now a senior at Burke High School.

Mose continued to express the importance of getting a good education. He would sometimes test my reading skills by having me read aloud a newspaper article that he felt I should know about. After I'd read the article, he would have me set it aside and think about what the writer was saying. Sometimes I could not recall what I had just read to him. It seemed that I was just saying the words without understanding them. Mose told me that I had to learn how to internalize what I was reading. He would sometimes ask me to write an essay on an article I had read. I told him that I did not know what an essay was. This had not been a requirement in my Special Education classes.

Mose never made me feel like an idiot because of my inability to read or write well; he simply encouraged me to try harder. Although I improved my grade point average, moving from D's and F's to C's and B's, I remained in the Special Education program throughout high school.

Mose disliked the fact that even though I acted like a gentleman, I hung out with the wrong people around the hotel and on the streets. For example, one Sunday morning I had to report to work at 8 a.m. Roy, one of the elderly Black bell staff, told me that a white female prostitute was staying in Room 205. He also told me to leave her alone or she might get me into trouble. Moments later, while Roy and I were still talking, the woman called down to the bellmen's station. Roy answered the phone. He wrote on a notepad that the guest needed a bucket of ice and handed the paper to me. He hung up the phone and told me that it was the prostitute, adding, "Take her the ice and hurry back down."

I went to the ice machine in the basement and filled the glass pitcher with ice. I took the elevator to the second floor and knocked on the door of Room 205. I heard a female saying, "Come on in." The door was unlocked so I opened it and went in. The occupant had brown hair and appeared to be in her 30s or 40s. I was surprised to see her lying on the bed wearing only a lacy, light blue nightgown. Even more surprising was that she was rubbing herself between her legs. I tried to avoid looking at her to let her know I was not interested, but as soon as I placed the ice on the table, she jumped up and ran to close the door. Then she smiled at me and I felt very nervous.

"Sit down," she told me. "I'm not going to bite you." Reluctantly, I sat on the bed. She sat beside me, too close for comfort. She offered me a drink, but I refused. "I'm working," I said. She told me she needed some money and would give me a blowjob for ten dollars. She moved still closer, again rubbing between her legs with one hand and squeezing her breasts with the other. I started to get hot and bothered so I stood up and started moving toward the door I told her I had to leave; she begged me not to go.

Just then, the phone rang. She answered it. I could hear the voice on the other end. It was Roy calling for me. She told him I had already left. When she hung up, she walked up to me and asked me if I would like to be her pimp. I asked her what I would be expected to do. She said I was to bring a john to her, and she would split the money with me. I thought about it for a moment. I knew of several white men in the hotel who were frequently looking for a woman. I also recalled the pimps in Atlantic City who had women selling their bodies for them. I could certainly use some extra money, so I agreed. I took so long getting back downstairs that Roy asked me what I was doing all that time. I lied and told him I was helping some other guests carry their luggage to their rooms.

Immediately I began thinking about two white men who were living in the hotel. They were constantly hounding me about finding them a prostitute. I never before considered helping them, but now I was ready to deliver. I wasn't sure, though, if they were still interested.

It was around 11:00 a.m. when Jake, a middle-aged white male resident of the hotel, with whom I had become friends, came downstairs to the lobby. Roy was outside waiting for some guests to arrive. I signaled to Jake. "Are you still looking for a prostitute?" I asked. He said he was. I asked how much he would be willing to give me.

"Ten dollars," he replied. I told him to wait while I made a phone call. I went into the bellmen's station, called the prostitute, and informed her that I had a customer who wanted her services. She told me to send him up to her room. I gave him her room number and told him to go on up. He headed for the elevator. Thirty minutes later he came back to the bellmen's station where I was standing. He was frowning.

"How was it?" I asked

He said, "That bitch can't screw. I didn't pay her."

"*What*?" I said, laughing. Both of us laughed awhile. Then I said, "She did give you her beautiful body. Maybe you didn't take full advantage of what she offered. You should have paid her even if you weren't satisfied. And you do need to give me the ten dollars you owe me." He took out a ten-dollar bill and gave it to me. Then he went to lunch. Right after he left, the phone rang. It was the prostitute. She complained to me about Jake's refusal to pay her. I didn't want to make her feel bad by telling her what he had told me; I only said that I was sorry for what had happened and that I would be up to see her on my break at 12:30.

When the time came, I took the back stairs to her room. I was scared as hell, but I knew I had to say something. I found her door unlocked. She was sitting on a chair. "I want to kill that cheapskate for having sex with me and then refusing to pay," she yelled.

"I'm so sorry," I apologized and gave her five dollars. "I hope this helps. But there is no way I can *force* him to pay." Then I advised her, "Next time, be sure to get the money *first*." When I left her, she was crying and clutching the money in her hand.

About an hour later, I saw her leaving the lobby. She didn't say anything to me but waved goodbye. I found out later that she checked out of the hotel the next morning. I was sorry that I had never asked her name. In spite of what had happened with my first experience as a pimp, I still felt that this was an easy way to make extra money.

Four months passed before I met another prostitute in the hotel. I saw a white woman in her early thirties with long blond hair sitting in the lobby. I went over to her and started a conversation. I found out that she had booked a room in the hotel on the third floor. Her name was Denise from a small country town in Oklahoma. She was on her way to Florida to start a new life after her recent divorce. Just before I left her to help a white man carry his luggage to his room, I told her that if she ever needed anything, to call me at the bellmen's station.

Later that evening, Mose answered the lobby telephone and told me to take ice to Room 315. When I knocked on the door with the ice, it was Denise, wearing white pajamas. I placed the ice bucket on the table, and she invited me to sit down and talk, but my boss was downstairs waiting for me. I promised her I'd come back when I got off duty at 11:00 p.m.

Normally after work, Mose and I would catch a cab home together, but that night I told him I had promised to wait for my brother Eddie to get off work at the Hyatt Regency Hotel as we were going somewhere together. When the white male clerk's back was turned, I ran up the front stairs to the second floor and took the back stairs to the third floor to Denise's room. She invited me in; I sat next to her on the bed. We drank rum and watched TV. After a while, she laid down, pulling the covers over her as she took off her pajamas. She began rubbing her feet against my back and asked, "Would you like to have sex with me?" I said I would. I got undressed and joined her in bed. We made love for hours as she taught me things that I had never done before. It was 5 a.m. when I finally left and caught a cab home. When I got home, my mother greeted me and asked why I was getting home so late. I lied and said it had been an unusually busy night and I had to work overtime.

At school the next day, I told a friend of mine, Pug, who was very knowledgeable about women what happened to me the night before. He asked me if Denise needed a pimp. I told him I'd find out. He also advised that I should read books by Iceberg Slim, if I was serious about being a pimp.

When I got to work, I found Denise sitting in the lobby, apparently waiting for me. After changing into my uniform, I joined her and suggested that we go outside to talk. When we left the lobby, she told me she was getting low on cash. I asked her if she wanted to do some tricks. She quickly answered, "Yes!" I informed her that I was now her pimp. We agreed that I would get her customers, and she would give me money after her third customer. By that time, she should have enough money to pay me. I told her to be sure she stayed in her room that evening.

That night and every night I worked thereafter; I asked every white man whose luggage I took up if he wanted a woman until I found one who did. I asked those who were not interested to not report me, or I would lose my job. The system worked. Denise made money and so did I — four hundred dollars in two weeks! Eventually Denise left for her new life in Florida, leaving me a note of goodbye.

Later a Black pimp I had met one night outside of the hotel introduced me to Angel, a Black prostitute. He was returning to New York and needed someone local to take over. We agreed on the terms and he left the next day. Angel was very difficult to work with; she lied all the time and tried to cheat me out of my money. But I couldn't complain because I feared getting fired. Nevertheless, I did make money because her customers tipped me very well. I got her over twenty customers in three weeks.

By April and May of '77, I had four prostitutes to come into my life, two Black and two white. The last one was Lisa. She had gotten kicked out of the hotel and asked me if I could send her some customers at another hotel down the street where she was staying. I told her I'd have to have sex with her first to see if she was any good. After I got off from work, I met her at the hotel, and we had sex. Satisfied with her performance, I agreed to be her pimp.

During that night, I noticed a burning sensation in my penis. Even after I finished bathing the next morning, my penis burned even worse. I went to school but had to leave early because I was in so much pain. I told my brother Eddie how I felt, and he said I should tell our sister Clarissa because she worked at the Medical University Hospital. I described to her the burning feeling, and she asked me if I had had unprotected sex with anyone. At first, I lied, but then I admitted that I had been with a prostitute the night before.

Without telling Mama, Clarissa called our family doctor who told her to have me come to his office right away. When he examined me, he told me that I had gonorrhea. He gave me a penicillin shot with the biggest needle I had ever seen. I ached for two days. After a shot like that, I promised myself I would never have sex with a prostitute again. It wasn't worth the money.

Three days later, I called Lisa and told her that I was through pimping. I advised her to get checked by a doctor right away. It was a wild and crazy ride. My bellhop pimping days were finally over and I was wiser for the experience.

CHAPTER 15

Twelfth Grade Problems

Often on Friday nights after work, I would join my friends on Bogard Street to hang out. On one Friday night, I couldn't find anyone I knew when I got there. Eddie had left home earlier, but I had no idea where he was. Eventually, I ran into an acquaintance who told me the boys were probably at a crab party at Masonic Temple Hall on St. Phillip Street. I should have known; during the summer, people in Charleston ate lots of crabs while they were still in season. When we got there, the place was crowded with young people I knew as well as older people who were sitting outside at tables eating crabs and drinking beer.

Pretty soon I ran into a girl named Mary; I was told that she was interested in me romantically. I knew her but wasn't interested in her that way. She walked over to me and asked me to buy her a beer. She seemed like she had already had too many, and I didn't want to be bothered with her. She kept begging for a beer, and she became so irritating that I finally told her to get the hell out of my face using a few choice words. She seemed hurt by my refusal, but I just didn't want to get involved with someone I wasn't interested in. I guess she got the point and moved on to talk to someone else.

It wasn't too long after that that I felt sharp pains in the back of my head, the left side of my face, and my left leg. When I was able to turn around, I saw a strange boy who I realized had just attacked me with a switchblade. I had no idea why since he didn't even know me. He probably would have continued if several of the older men hadn't grabbed him and pulled him away from me. I quickly left to look for my brother and some of my friends. I wasn't aware that I was bleeding profusely, but when Eddie saw me and asked, "What happened to you?" I realized that there was blood all over me. My first instinct was to go back and beat the man up, but I was beginning to feel weak from the loss of blood. I knew I needed to go to the emergency room. Some time passed before I found out that the boy who had attacked me was a close friend of Mary's and that she must have told him how I had insulted her. At any rate, the men had held him until the police arrived. I pressed charges and he was arrested. Before his case came up in court, I saw him walking down the street to the courthouse where I too was headed. He offered me a hundred dollars to drop the charges, but I refused, and he was sentenced to spend some time in jail.

After summer vacation ended, I broke up with the girl I had been going with because she was never willing to go beyond a kiss, and I wanted more than that from a relationship. Occasionally I would run into Lisa; she was in my brother Eddie's class, and she seemed eager to carry on a conversation with me instead of just speaking. The conversations gradually became more personal to the point that I realized she liked me. I got the idea that she was interested in going beyond kissing. When I showed interest in being her boyfriend, she broke up with the boy she had been going with, and we started doing some serious loving. Sometimes we would skip school and go to her house and have sex while her parents were at work.

On the night of the prom, my sister Mamie drove Lisa and me to dinner at a fine restaurant for a steak dinner and then to the prom and left us there at the school. She was supposed to pick us up later, but Lisa and I left the prom early and went to a motel where I had made reservations. I called Mamie to tell her she needn't pick us up because we would catch a cab home.

As soon as we entered the room, we began to get undressed, but before we got in bed the telephone rang. I answered, but there was no response. Lisa got scared, assuming that it was her mother calling, but her mother knew nothing about our whereabouts. I did everything possible to calm her fears. I assured her that the call was intended for someone else and the operator had called the wrong room, but she would not be comforted. She got dressed and insisted that we leave right away. I got angry because I had spent over a hundred dollars for two hours in the room, and now we were leaving without having sex.

Nevertheless, we continued seeing each other, and her parents seemed to like me. Sometimes I had dinner with them on the nights I didn't have to work. I felt that I was in love with Lisa and even considered asking her to marry me. Everything was going smoothly, I thought, until Lisa suddenly disappeared without telling me. Her mother said she was visiting out of town relatives, but I couldn't understand why she didn't let me know her plans. As weeks went by, I became more and more puzzled because she never contacted me.

When I learned that she was back home, I was very happy and rode my bike to her house one Sunday morning expecting to have a wonderful reunion and an explanation of her absence. Instead, when she saw me get off my bike, she started hitting me for no apparent reason. I tried to hold her hands, but she got them loose and started crying while hitting me in the face again. When I asked her why she was angry with me, she didn't say a word. In desperation, I got back on my bike and went back home completely puzzled. Convinced that I would never get an explanation, I never went back to her house and when we ran into each other at school, we never spoke.

It was months before I found out the truth. She had assumed that I used protection whenever we had sex and I did not. She left town because she was pregnant and her mother insisted that she have an abortion. I realized that we were not ready to have a family, and her mother had made a wise decision, although not one of Lisa's choosing. I never had unprotected sex with anyone after that.

CHAPTER 16

Yielding to Temptation

After a delicious dinner one Sunday in 1977, I got ready to go to work at the Francis Marion Hotel. As I was leaving, my mother gave me twenty dollars and asked me to stop at the corner drugstore and buy Daddy some batteries. I could have stopped after work but didn't want to take a chance on forgetting. So, on my way to work I rode my bike to the drugstore.

Before I could get to the section where the batteries were, I passed another department where I noticed some things that I needed for myself but kept forgetting to buy. However, the only money I had in my pocket was the twenty dollars my mother had given me. I don't know what got into me because I knew better, but I decided to go back to the counter where the small batteries were and put them into my pocket without paying for them. Then after work, I could come back and buy what I needed for myself. As soon as I stole the batteries, I left the store and headed for my bike, but the white security guard had followed me and stopped me from leaving. I should have known better because Black customers were always watched more carefully than white ones, assuming they were more likely to steal.

And I had played right into his hands. He had seen me put the batteries in my pocket and held out his hand, demanding that I give them back, which I did. I thought that was the end of it and proceeded toward the pole where my bike was, thinking I could unlock it and continue on to work.

"Not so fast, young man," he said. "You're going back into the store with me and wait for the police." My first impulse was to run, but I didn't want to leave my brand-new bike behind. I had no choice but to go with him.

By the time the police arrived, several people who evidently heard the conversation had gathered near the door. I was terribly embarrassed when I recognized that several of them were my neighbors. I gave one of the guys I knew my bicycle key and asked him to unlock it and take it back to my house.

I called my mother from jail and told her what had happened. I begged her to come and get me. I could hear her talking to my father in the background. Shortly she told me that Daddy was not sympathetic, and I would have to stay locked up and take my medicine like a man. I was miserable sitting in that narrow cell, even if it was for just one night.

I had a lot of time to think. I realized how stupid I had been since this was my second time in jail although the first time, I was not guilty. On the first occasion, two of my friends and I were walking home from a party. We were stopped by a white policeman. He got out of his car and asked us where we were going. Then he began to search us. I had a silver key chain in my pocket that my brother had given me a week before. The officer found it and asked me where I got it. I told him the truth, but he didn't believe me. He said that someone had broken into a salesman's car and stolen some items and this key chain looked like one of them. He arrested me for possession of stolen property. I spent the whole weekend in the new jail the city had just built. On Monday morning, the judge released me, saying the officer had made a false arrest. A Black detective who knew my family advised my mother that she should hire a lawyer and sue the city, but we didn't have the money. I never did get my silver key chain back.

Now here I was in jail again, and this time I was guilty. How quickly we forget! I promised myself that I would never steal anything again. Early the next morning a guard woke me up, opened the cell gate, and told me to follow him to the judge. The judge charged me only with a minor misdemeanor and said I would have to pay a fine within thirty days. I breathed a sigh of relief. To this day I have never done anything else that would cause me to be arrested.

CHAPTER 17

Move to Atlanta

In June 1977, on the day of my graduation from Burke High School, I stood around with my classmates in the parking lot of County Hall conversing and waiting for our homeroom teachers to line us up for the procession. Since my last name was Alston, I expected to be near the beginning of the line, but instead I was put near the end. When I inquired, I was told that the students who had received scholarships to college were first in line and the Special Education students like me were placed after them. I was disappointed and surprised to be singled out like that as one of the dummies! Instead of feeling proud to be graduating, I felt like crying. My family members had no idea how embarrassed I felt and were proud of me anyhow.

All summer long I wondered what I could do with my life now that I was no longer a student. Most of my classmates were going to college or into military service. I knew I would not be accepted in any college so I took the entrance exams for the Army and Navy. I didn't pass either one. An elderly Black man who worked part-time in the hotel parking lot told me that he was a reserve in the Merchant Marines and offered to try to get me a job on a ship. That sounded wonderful since I wanted to travel and see the world, but he never followed through on his promise.

One day I talked to my father about how hopeless I felt. "Don't give up so easily," he told me. "Something good is waiting for you. Just continue to work at the hotel, save your money and wait for God's guidance. He won't forsake you." I wanted to believe him, but as the weeks and months went by, I became impatient. I was no longer a bellman but was in training as a painter. Even so, I was still working at the hotel, and that was not what I wanted to do for the rest of my life. I realized that I would have to take my future into my own hands and make a change.

By August it occurred to me that remaining in Charleston was futile, and since my sister, Annette lived in Atlanta, I might have a better chance at a good career if I moved in with her. I told my girlfriend Fredricka of my decision. She thought it was a good idea. She was preparing to go to college and assured me of her support, adding that we would stay in touch and we would get together again at some time in the future.

When I told Daddy of my decision, pending Annette's approval, he thought it was a good idea, but my mother thought I was moving too fast. I assured her that Annette was the best person to help me get my life together. Mama called Annette for her opinion, and my sister approved of my plan; she said she would be happy to have me live with her. Reluctantly, my mother gave up her opposition and accepted my plan to move to Atlanta in November. By that time, I would have saved enough money for the move.

Two days before Thanksgiving, Annette came home for a visit. She advised me to buy some heavy winter clothes because Atlanta was getting cold. I said goodbye to all of my friends. It was most difficult to bid my girlfriend a reluctant farewell since I was really in love with her and going our separate ways would not be easy. I realized that her intentions were good but that realistically things would never be the same between us. Saying goodbye to my parents, four sisters and two brothers living in Charleston was very emotional. My mother was upstairs in bed with a blanket over her head; she would not even let me kiss her goodbye . Still I knew that leaving my native city was something I had to do if I wanted to make something of my life. Annette and I left the house together.

It was midnight when our Delta airplane arrived in Atlanta. We were greeted by snow and the coldest night that I had ever experienced. Annette and I got our luggage and caught a cab to her apartment on Boltic Road.

The following Saturday morning we took a bus downtown so that my sister could show me around. I was amazed how far from downtown Boltic Road was and how hilly the streets were. After lunch we went grocery shopping. She told me I would have to learn how to cook because she was not going to be my mother.

We had a cousin, Arthur, who had been living with Annette, but he had recently moved to his own place. All that weekend I just sat around the apartment watching TV, smoking marijuana, drinking wine, and listening to album after album of music I liked.

The following Monday morning I got up when I heard Annette in the shower preparing to go to work. She was an assistant teacher at a school downtown. I was to leave with her and, while she was working, I would be looking for a job. After breakfast she gave me a set of keys to the apartment and wrote down directions on how to catch the bus to and from the apartment. We left together. It was rush hour and the bus was crowded. When we got to her stop, she rang the bell, kissed me on the cheek, and wished me luck on my search for a job. Most of the people on board got off at the Marietta Street stop. I got off, too, as she had instructed me. Annette had told me to go to Peachtree Street first, but I didn't know how to get there, and all the streets seemed long and endless. I remembered my brother once warning me that, when I was in a strange place, I should never act as if I didn't know where I was going because strangers sometimes got robbed. Therefore, I tried to look as if I knew where I was going, but I had difficulty reading and pronouncing some of the street signs and realized that my inability to read well presented a big challenge.

I eventually got to a small park on Peachtree Street. It was a very busy street with people everywhere. I couldn't help noticing one particular building. It was very tall and appeared to be covered in glass. I had never seen such a beautiful building before. As I walked closer, I noticed a sign on the door that read "The Peachtree Plaza." I went inside. It was as beautiful inside as it was outside. I asked the first person I saw what kind of building it was. She looked at me as if I should have known. "It's a hotel, of course," she said, "the Peachtree Plaza Hotel." I thanked her and got the idea that, since I was accustomed to working at a hotel in Charleston, I might be able to get a job there as a bellman. I kept walking around the hotel with a feeling of awe. When I saw an elevator, I decided to get on it and see what other wonders existed on different floors. The operator must have guessed that I had never been there before and told me I should ride to the top floor where I would get an excellent view of the entire city. The elevator had glass windows. The view became more and more beautiful the higher we went. "This is the top floor," the operator told me. "There's a wonderful restaurant here where you might want to have lunch."

"I think I will," I said, and thanked her. I ordered two glasses of Coca Cola as the restaurant revolved, providing changing views of the city below. I finally remembered that I was there to see if I could get a job but didn't know where the personnel office was. Looking through a first-floor window, I saw another tall building close by and five Black men moving boxes. I left the hotel and ran in their direction. I asked one of them where I could apply for a job, and he directed me to the back of the building where many more people were moving boxes, desks, and chairs. One of them told me to go to the small office he pointed to. Once inside, I saw a woman sitting at a desk typing. I introduced myself and told her I needed a job. She gave me an application to fill out and showed me a chair where I could sit.

After she read the completed application, she asked me if I could start work right away. I said I could. I felt blessed to be able to find a job so easily, but I had no idea what the job was. Moments later a big-muscled Black man came into the office. The woman at the desk instructed him to take me upstairs to work. The man introduced himself as Joe. He said, "You gonna work in *those* clothes? Do you realize how dirty you're gonna get?"

I said, "It's okay. I need the work." He shrugged and told me to follow him.

"And keep on your coat," he added. You'll be going outside and coming back in a lot, and you won't have time to change." I followed Joe around the corner to the back elevator which we took to the 29th floor. Down the hall we found two young men and a third older man whom he called "Reverend." They were moving chairs and desks. One of the men looked at me and said, "Man, you gonna get really dirty in those clothes." Nobody had told me ahead of time what kind of work I would be doing and I thought I'd be all right.

"It's okay," I said. "I really need this job and had no idea I would get it so easily."

He replied, "Ain't nothin' easy about this job."

As I watched the two men lifting desks and chairs and moving them down the hall where they loaded them onto the elevator, I realized that my new job would consist of a lot of heavy lifting. As a man known as "Reverend" and I started to work, I found myself really struggling. Occasionally the younger men would lend us a hand. After a while, Joe assigned Reverend and me to carry a lot of empty boxes and trash outside. The boxes had to be put in a recycle container and the trash had to be dumped in a big trash can. Each time we went outside, I got colder and dirtier. At the end of the day I asked Joe if that would be my job every day. He said yes, that would be my permanent duty. My back was aching from all that lifting, and I was so cold, dirty, and tired that I knew I couldn't go through another day like that. As much as I needed a job, I shook hands with Joe and told him I quit.

When I got home, I told Annette what had happened. She got an attitude and showed her displeasure. Then she called Mama and told her I had quit my first job. Mama told her to send me back home. I got on the phone and told Mama I was not going back to Charleston. Atlanta was the right place for me. My mother hung up on me before I finished explaining. Annette did not fix me dinner that night and told me I was on my own. She didn't have anything more to say to me. I fixed myself two cold baloney sandwiches and went to bed early.

For the rest of the week I just sat around the apartment and listened to Annette when she got home complain that I was wasting my time when I should be looking for a job.

Annette's best friend was a woman who worked at the school where she did. She was married to a minister, Rev. Williams. They treated my sister like a member of their own family and often took her with them wherever they went. She had made many friends through The Williamse, and she could depend on them for help whenever she needed something. Annette had become a member of their church and attended regularly. The last place I wanted to go was church, even though my early life included occasional church attendance. We were not very religious, in spite of the fact that my great-grandfather co-founded Vanderhorst Memorial CME Church on 66 Hanover Street in Charleston. We were members but did not attend regularly. My great-grandfather's wife, Mamie J. Simmons continued to function in church until she died at the age of 99.

At Annette's insistence, I went with her to Rev. Williams' church the second week that I was in Atlanta. When we got there, the service had already started and the people were shouting and singing in the spirit. I liked what I heard. After church the minister and his wife invited Annette and me to dinner at their home. After a tasty meal, the women went to the kitchen to clean up while Rev. Williams and I sat in the living room watching football and discussing what I wanted to do with my life. He said he didn't want to push religion on me, but I should consider attending church regularly. Then he told me that he had arranged for Clark College to hire me as a janitor. He said employment at a college might lead to better things. As an employee I would have the option of taking a class every semester.

The next day I got up early with Annette and put on my best suit. She gave me directions to the college and wrote down the numbers of the buses I needed to take. When I arrived on the campus, I was tremendously impressed to see so many young brothers and sisters attending college. I kept on walking until I found the little green building Rev. Williams had described to me the night before. He said I would find a man named Mr. Anderson there.

Several people were standing near the entrance. I asked if they could direct me to Mr. Anderson's office. "I'm Mr. Anderson," one of them said. "Are you the young man Rev. Williams sent for the janitor's job?" I introduced myself and we shook hands. He looked me up and down, then said, "You look like you should be in one of these college classes, not working as a janitor." I told him I would like to enter college, but I needed to make some money first. He said that if I did a good job as a janitor he would see that I got in school. He made me feel good about going to college, but I still was not sure that I was college material. Mr. Anderson told me that the woman and other man standing next to him would be my supervisors. Then he led me into his office. His secretary gave me an application to fill out. After I completed it, Mr. Anderson had the other man take me to Bradley Hall, the men's dormitory where I was assigned to work. After being told what my job entailed I was sent home. Mr. Anderson said I was too well dressed to start work that day and that I should arrive by eight o'clock the next morning dressed more appropriately.

I went home feeling happy. Annette was very happy for me, too. She cooked me dinner that night but threatened to send me back to Charleston if I quit this job.

I went to work the next day and every day thereafter and tried to do the best job possible. Over a period of time, I learned to love my job and many of the brothers and sisters I met from all across the United States, Africa and the islands. The brothers in my dorm thought that I was a student janitor because, when I was not working, I was sitting down under a tree reading a book by a Black author. By the end of the semester, some of the students were giving me books by Black authors that they had read, thinking I might enjoy them, too. I was particularly impressed with *The Life and Times of Frederick Douglass*. It was hard reading for me, but I took that book with me everywhere I went. I was determined to learn about how Douglass was able to liberate himself from slavery. I was becoming conscious and proud of my Black heritage. I even changed my name to Kamubu, a name I got from the song "Kamubuca." I also tried to appear intelligent so that the students would think I was working as a janitor only temporarily. I had dreams of becoming great one day. As time went by, several of the brothers told me that I was their inspiration. On my break I would visit Morehouse College,

Spelman College, Morris Brown College, and Atlanta University. I spent a lot of time in the Atlanta University library because I had heard that the great Black scholar, Dr. W.E.B. Du Bois had taught at that campus many years ago.

I had been working at Clark College for about six months, never missing a day, when Mr. Anderson told me I could enroll in a summer class. I decided to take a class in typing because I was interested in becoming a writer. I mistakenly enrolled in an advanced typing class and had a very hard time keeping up. The teacher insisted on speed and accuracy, but since I was sitting in the back of the room, it took her a while to notice how slow I was. Eventually, however, she did observe me and told me I needed to be in a class for beginners. The next day I enrolled in Typing I. but did not find it helpful. The male teacher spent more time talking to his female students about their personal problems than teaching us how to type. After two days I realized I was wasting my time and dropped the class. I used some of the money I had earned to buy my own typewriter and started teaching myself to type at home.

I knew that my greatest challenge to success was still to overcome my illiteracy and in spite of the books I had read, I had not made much progress. One day when I was on campus, I noticed a flier advertising a community center on the south side of Atlanta that taught adult education. I took the flier home to discuss with Annette at dinner. She told me she knew where the center was and thought it was a great idea for me to check into it. I immediately left the dinner table and called the number on the flier. I told the receptionist that I was interested in the adult education program. She said they were still enrolling students and I should come to talk with one of the teachers. The next day after work, I caught the bus to the center and easily found the office. I was warmly greeted by two Black female employees. I told them that I was new in town and wanted to enroll in the adult education program. One asked, "Is there anything in particular that you want to study?"

"Yes, I want to learn how to read and write better. Right now, I'm working at Clark College. I'm allowed to take some classes, but I don't think I'm advanced enough to take college classes. If I could improve my reading and writing, I would be able to make a better living than a janitor's salary. Also, I want to be a writer and I can't accomplish that goal with my present skills.

One of the ladies took me back to the room to enroll. From her helpful attitude, I knew we would get along well. "I am going to be your new teacher," she said. When she tested my reading, writing and math skills, she told me that I was functioning on the ninth-grade level. "Come back every Tuesday and Thursday and I'll soon have you ready to take college level classes." I promised her I would.

I went to the adult evening classes for ten weeks without fail, from February through the third week of April 1978. There was another young man in my class, but all he wanted to learn was enough to get his driver's license. Whenever the teacher was not around, I would question him about why he didn't want to learn more, but he didn't seem interested. After he felt he was ready to take his test, I never saw him again. I guess he passed and got his license. Then it was just my teacher and me. Each time we met she would question me on the previous lessons. I made learning my highest priority and spent all of my time when I wasn't working studying history, math, and science, which I really enjoyed. My teacher liked the fact that I was a serious student and was making progress. Nevertheless, I told her I was still having trouble pronouncing some of the street names. She advised me to write down the names of the streets I was having trouble with so that she could help me. I added other words I had trouble pronouncing. After a while my list contained hundreds of words.

As I was mopping the third-floor hall at Clark College on Good Friday, Jeff, one of the students I had gotten to know, came out of his room and said, "Hey, Kumuba, are you going to the Morehouse auditorium to hear Minister Louis Farrakhan?"

"Who is he?" I asked. "I've never heard of him."

"He's one of the leaders of the Honorable Elijah Muhammad and the Black Muslims," he replied. Moving closer to me, he said, "Kumuba, you need to check this brother out. He was trained by Malcolm X himself." I was impressed, for I certainly had heard of Malcolm X. "I'll be there on my lunch break."

It was 12:15 when I was able to get there, and the program had already started. The auditorium was packed with Black students, but I finally found an empty seat. I was very disappointed to learn that I had missed Minister Farrakhan's speech, and now students were going up to the microphone in the front to ask questions about the Nation of Islam. I had no previous knowledge of such a nation and found it difficult to understand what they were talking about. What I did remember was that Minister Farrakhan said he was going to rebuild the Black Nation of Islam. As I was leaving the meeting, a Black female student next to me said, "Too bad you missed the speech, but he's going to speak again tomorrow evening at a dinner at Morris Brown College. If you want to hear him the sister over there is selling tickets for fifteen dollars." I went in the direction she pointed me to and bought a ticket.

I still had time for lunch, so I started walking down Ashby Street in the Westend in the hope of finding a fast food restaurant nearby. I eventually saw a tall white building on Gordon Street with a sign on top: "Shrine of the Black Madonna's Nursery, Cultural Center and Southern Regional Office." It sounded interesting, so I walked in that direction. The windows were filled with African artifacts. Through the window I could see a young Black woman with a small afro behind the counter. She was holding a baby in her arms. Our eyes met and she signaled me to come inside. She greeted me pleasantly and invited me to look around the store and feel at home. I thought she might have been African but didn't feel it would be polite to ask. I saw many African items that I wanted to buy but I had to get back to work and purchased only an African hat for twenty dollars. As I was leaving, I asked the lady her name. She said it was Ada. "It's an African name," she explained, "given to me by my church."

"Where is your church?" I asked. "It's right next door— The Shrine of the Black Madonna. What is your name?"

I answered, "Kumuba."

"Why don't you come to my church next Sunday? It's Easter, and I promise you you'll feel right at home."

"Thanks for the invitation," I said, rushing out the door for work. "I think I will."

Remembering the dinner where Minister Louis Farrakhan would speak, I got up early the next morning and headed downtown to look for a tape recorder so I could tape his speech. After visiting several stores unsuccessfully, I finally found one in a pawn shop and bought it. From there I went back to the Shrine of the Black Madonna Cultural Center and Bookstore and bought some incense. Outside I saw several young Black men wearing identical white t-shirts and blue jeans. Nearby was another man who looked like he might have been a security guard standing in front of what I assumed was the church. I noticed a round-headed cross on the building. I later learned that this unusual cross was Egyptian and was called an ankh, symbolizing life and power. I introduced myself to the guard and asked him if I could go inside the church to see what it looked like. He looked me up and down and assuming that I meant no harm, I guess, said that he'd go in with me. He told me his name was Tacumba.

I did not expect the sanctuary to be so beautiful. I was completely in awe. On each wall were big, striking African murals. Tacumba told me the symbols represented the struggle of Black people for freedom in both ancient and modern times. One picture near the altar was a tall Black man Tacumba said was Mose. Another picture was of a tall Black woman holding a small child. Tacumba identified them as The Black Madonna holding the baby Jesus. "Are you telling me that Mary and Jesus were Black?" I asked in amazement.

"Yes," he answered, "just like you and me. If you study ancient history, you'll know that this is true. The ancient paintings of the Madonna and child were always Black until Michelangelo and the European Renaissance artists began painting the Madonna and child White. What precious secrets were revealed to me that Saturday afternoon! I walked away from the Shrine with a voice in my head saying, "The truth will set me free."

I arrived around 7:00 p.m. on the campus of Morris Brown and entered the auditorium where about three hundred people were being served dinner. Some were already seated, and others were standing in the serving line. The Muslim brothers were dressed in blue and black suits. I handed one of them my ticket. He patted me down for weapons, then told me to go and enjoy myself. I got in the serving line and got a dinner plate, filling it with food as the line moved forward. I looked around to find an empty seat and saw one next to a woman; I asked if it was taken. She said it was not and patted the chair inviting me to join her. Minister Louis Farrakhan was sitting up front surrounded by other Muslims. He was wearing a gold two-piece suit. After everyone had finished eating, Minister Louis Farrakhan was introduced and he walked to the podium to speak. Before he could say a word, all hell broke loose in the back of the auditorium as two Black men began fighting. Women were screaming and there was all kinds of commotion. In the front, Minister Farrakhan was being protected by a group of bodyguards who stood in front and around him. Eventually the two men were separated and escorted out of the building.

Once all was calm again, Minister Louis Farrakhan began to speak but was immediately interrupted by a respectful audience that stood up and applauded him. After the long applause, he directed us to take our seats. I turned on my tape recorder, which I remembered to bring. He greeted us in the Arabic words, "As-salamu alaykum. (God's peace be upon you)" The audience responded with "Walaikum Salam (And unto you peace)." He excited the audience for about two hours as he spoke without notes about Black history and the struggle of today. I was deeply impressed. I had never in my life heard anyone speak as he did except on the tapes of Malcolm X that I had listened to in Charleston. One of the things that he said that has stayed with me even to this day was "You don't drink, you don't smoke, you don't fornicate, but if you don't do anything for the liberation of Black people, then all your good is meaningless." After the program, I, like many of the others in the audience, went up front to shake hands with this amazing leader. Then I went home in a daze. He had painted the struggle of Black people permanently in my mind. I knew I had to do something for my people, but I had no clue as to where to begin. I realized I had a lot of thinking to do.

CHAPTER 18

Conversion

The morning after I heard and taped Minister Louis Farrakhan's inspiring speech, I woke up early and listened to it over and over. Eventually Annette was awakened by the sound and came to my room to find out whose voice I was listening to. When I told her, she asked, "How come you're listening to the same speech? Are you going to become a Black Muslim now?" I answered that I was not because the minister did not ask anyone to join the Nation of Islam, but I had never heard any other Black man talk like that, and I found him fascinating.

It was Easter Sunday and Annette invited me to go with her to Rev. Williams's church. I thanked her but said I had been invited to services at the Shrine of the Black Madonna. "Okay, Brother X," she said sarcastically. "Have it your way," and left my room. After we had eaten breakfast, we both got dressed and went our separate ways.

From my Dogwood Tree apartment near Bankhead Road I caught the bus that Easter Sunday morning to Clark College and ran the two miles to the Shrine of the Black Madonna. WEST END The Shrine was two blocks from the church of civil rights leader Rev. Ralph Abernathy. I arrived at the church at 11:15 A.M. A young Black woman with a beautiful afro greeted me at the door. I went inside and signed the church guest list, then entered the sanctuary and took a seat. I noticed that a lot of people in the congregation wore red shirts or blouses and black pants or skirts. Some wore black two-piece suits and red shirts, which were the same colors that I had on.

The service started with a period of meditation followed by the choir singing, "Rise nation rise, praise God the Black Nation shall rise." They marched from the back to the front of the sanctuary; the congregation stood and joined the singing. The choir members sat in the reserved front seats after marching in. Then a lady who had taken her place on the altar stood and welcomed everyone to the Shrine. I later learned that she was one of the church's secretaries. Her name is Fundi Anika Sala. Fundi is a Swahili word meaning skilled in one's trade. After her invocation and prayer, she instructed everyone to stand and recite the church's Creed that was printed on the back of the church bulletin. She instructed the congregation to remain standing to sing "Life Every Voice and Sing." At the end of the song everyone raised their fists in the air. Afterward the choir and congregation began to sing again. I felt the presence of the Holy Spirit as I had never felt it before and I surrendered to the Spirit.

After the offering was taken and blessed, the choir rose to sing again. The selection was "I Stood on the Banks of Jordan." Some of the women in the congregation reacted with screams and shouts. As I listened, I thought of Africans on slave ships chained so close together they couldn't move as they crossed the Atlantic Ocean to the islands and the shores of North America. I found myself wiping tears from my eyes.

Then Bishop Sondai Nyerere (Donald Lester) rose to preach. In spite of his attire, he reminded me more of a revolutionary leader than a traditional Black preacher. He spoke on many of the issues that Minister Farrakhan had discussed the night before. He said that Israel was a nation of Black African people and that there were many references in the Bible to the race of the Israelites. He cited several specific examples. He told us that King David was a Black man, as was his son, King Solomon, and that Jesus was a direct descendent of Solomon. He also said that Mary, the mother of Jesus, was Black, as were many of the major prophets. This was my first time hearing that God is not a man but a Divine Spirit. I was convinced that all he said was true.

Then he began discussing the serious problems that Black people in America and around the world have that require major changes. He explained why we need to build economic, political, and institutional power for ourselves. He said that this was the only way the Black race could be liberated from White oppression. What really touched a nerve in me were his words, "We should be tired of mopping and cleaning after others when there is so much work we need to do for ourselves." Throughout his sermon there was much applause.

He preached such an inspiring sermon that when he said, "The church is now open for anyone who wants to join in the struggle." I was the first to walk down the aisle. I don't know what moved me to join; all I knew was that I loved what this church stood for. About twenty more people followed me down the aisle and joined the Shrine that day. We were all told to face the audience to be recognized as new members. We were led upstairs to the church office where we were told of our requirements and completed the necessary paper work. I had no reluctance at all to do whatever I needed to do to participate. I was fully committed.

CHAPTER 19

Commitment

After joining the church, I was interviewed and escorted into another room where established members interacted with new ones as we enjoyed refreshments. As a new member, I was instructed that the use of any drugs other than those prescribed by a doctor was forbidden. I was glad that somebody was going to help me quit smoking marijuana because I wanted to stop anyway, but before today, I had no compelling reason. Now I did.

Joining the Shrine of the Black Madonna required me to make some commitments and sacrifices for the church. One of the female officials named Nailah told me that if I was serious about changing my lifestyle, I had to participate fully in the church's program. She also said that I could participate on the church's general membership level if I chose to. General membership is reserved for those who attend church not only on Sundays but during the week as well. I wanted to work on personal change, so I agreed to attend week-night classes and other church functions regularly after work, even if it meant being late for dinner. It was clear that the church was disciplined and committed to programming for the liberation of Black people. Other than the Black Muslims, I had never met a group of Black people who were that serious. The first step was to attend the church's orientation the next night at 7:15 p. m.

A lady asked me if I was driving or if I needed a ride home. "I'm taking the bus," I answered. She motioned to one of the brothers. "Juma can drive you home," she said. "You don't need to take the bus."

"That'll be great," I said, "but first I want to stop by the Cultural Center to purchase a copy of the book, *The Black Messiah and Black Christian Nationalism: New Directions for the Black Church* by the Shrine's founder, Rev. Albert B. Cleage."

"I'll be happy to wait for you," he replied.

As Juma was driving me home, I told him how fascinated I was with the church service. I had never heard a minister preach about building power for Black people other than Malcolm X and Minister Louis Farrakhan. Most preachers I had heard were just interested in getting money and then sending people off to heaven somewhere. The Shrine was different. The money that this church collected was for the building of institutional power for Black people.

When I got back to my apartment, Annette was cooking dinner. I told her I had joined the Shrine of the Black Madonna. "What kind of church is that?" she asked. I told her that the Shrine is a church that works to improve the social, political and economic conditions of Black people. Sarcastically, she said, "Oh yeah, I'd sure like to see that. Now you really got a job on your hands."

I replied, "If we don't try to help our people, then who would?"

"Brother, you go right on ahead and help Black people. But first sit down and let me feed you." I kissed her on the cheek and went to my room to change clothes.

After work the next day, I showered and changed clothes, then caught the bus to Clark College and walked from there to the Shrine of the Black Madonna to attend the orientation session. Again, everyone except me and some other new members wore red and black. Orientation was exciting. The congregation sang songs as part of the Rite of Passage for members who had completed basic training and were now moving up to the advanced training level. Everyone was excited for the twelve candidates who emerged from the back of the sanctuary carrying candles. One of the ministers asked each candidate to approach the altar. Each candidate was instructed to kneel and pray silently for God to forgive him of his past sins against Black people. Then the candidates were instructed to stand and repeat ritual vows. One of the ministers held incense and a candle in her hand, followed by baptism by symbolic fire. After the ritual a few more ministers came up and gave the candidates the official right hand of fellowship.

The congregation sang as the candidates returned to their seats. Bishop Sondai (the minister who had preached during the church service) stood and began his lecture. He explained that the church is the instrument of God on earth and that our church's mission is to liberate Black people. But first, he said Black people had to change their *niggerized minds*. He said that without loyalty, commitment, and a clearly defined chain of command, the Black man would forever be locked in oppression. The chain of slavery, he continued, had been removed from our bodies and placed on our minds, and the white slave masters still controlled our minds. He told us Black people needed a new way of thinking to serve our own best interest. No one, he said, "Was going to give Black people power; we had to earn it ourselves through our own hard work."

Before closing his lecture, he read a quotation from *The Miseducation of the Negro,* a book by Carter G. Woodson. "If you can control a man's thinking, you do not have to worry about his actions. When a man feels that he is inferior, you do not have to compel him to accept an inferior status for he seeks it himself. If you make a man think that he is justly an outcast, you do not have to order him to the back door. He will go without being told, and if there is no back door, his very nature will demand one."

When the orientation was over, two brothers and a sister walked over to greet me. They introduced themselves as Captain Mwando, Mwalimu Sekou, and his wife Fundi Morenike. Captain Mwando informed me that he would be our group leader, and the other two would be his assistants. He asked me to follow him to the back of the sanctuary where several new members were seated. He introduced us. Each member gave me a fellowship hug. The group made me feel very comfortable as I sat listening to the information that Captain Mwando shared. We were informed that the Shrine's national office and headquarters were in Detroit, with other Michigan locations in Kalamazoo and Flint. There was also a Shrine in Houston, Texas.

I remembered hearing Bishop Sondai say, "The church can't build power with ignorant Black people. The leadership vanguard for Black people must be intelligent and it must set an example for other Black people to follow." Everyone I met seemed intelligent, and I knew I had to learn how to read better. I felt inspired by all the great possibilities that I was learning about. There was so much that I needed to learn that I stopped attending my nightly adult education class. It was far more important to attend classes at the Shrine.

During these classes I learned about Africa and the Pan-African world. I watched other members taking notes and tried to do it myself for a while, but since writing was such a challenge for me, I eventually put down my notebook and began learning by listening. The more I listened the more eager I was to buy the books that were required for the class. While I was not making any progress in writing, my reading skills were improving.

I read so much during the following month that my mind felt overworked to the extent that I even considered taking a vacation from the Shrine to give it a rest. I did stop attending for a few days. Then one day during my lunch hour, I met a Black woman who had been hired as a janitor at Clark College. She told me that she was a Jehovah's Witness. What she said about her religion really confused me because it was so different from what I had learned. She made it sound that God was some old white man who would come down from heaven and destroy the earth by fire. I began to understand that religion could be quite complex without the proper interpretation. I realized that I needed to go back to my classes at the Shrine and talk to someone for clarification.

I talked to one of the ministers, Mwalimu Tarik. The Swahili word Mwalimu means teacher. I told him about the problems I was having with religion. I read the passage from John 3:16 in the Bible: "God so loved the world that He gave His only begotten Son..."

"I am aware of the scriptures," he said. "The problem is that some people take one scripture and build their entire denomination on it instead of on the Bible as a whole. The Bible is a covenant between God and the Black nation Israel," he continued. "The people in the Bible struggled to maintain that relationship, which is not easy to do. God sent Mose, the prophets, the Black Messiah Jesus and many others. But Israel was a stiff-necked people at the time, the same as Black people are today. Change is not easy. You have to be patient. The church teaches the science of Kua. It will help you become what you already are." I stayed for Bible class that night and continued to attend classes at the Shrine.

Six months after I proved myself ready for leadership, I was selected, along with eleven other new members for basic training under the leadership of Bishop Lindiwe (Stovall Lester) and several others. I was given my new African name, Dadisi (inquisitive) Mwende (one who desires) Netifnet (freedom). Basic training lasted sixteen weeks. I learned the dynamics of the group process and began to understand God to be cosmic energy and creative intelligence in which we live, move, and have our being. My group assignments were to study and understand the church Creed, Teaching, Philosophy, and Program. In addition, we study the Jerusalem Bible because that Bible had more books than the King James Version. Members of the Shrine are Orthodox Christians who follow in the footsteps of the Revolutionary Black Messiah Jesus.

We attend African history class at night taught by our group leaders Bishop Lindiwe, Bishop Ayanna Abi-Kyles and Bishop Kimathi. We had to learn all the countries in Africa. I was fascinated about learning about the great Empires of Africa—Songhai Empire, Mali Empire, Empire Ghana, Ethiopian Empire, Mossi Kingdoms and Benin Empire. We also learned about Marcus Garvey and the Universal Negro Improvement Association UNIA. Colonel Zizwe taught a Tuesday evening class called "Realities of A New Era" in which we were instructed to read the Newspapers, Newsweek and Time Magazines. He said, "A Black revolutionary must be informed about the plight of his people. Then the revolutionary had to prepare him or herself as a group for some programmatic action against their oppression."

A big part of the group process was that I had to invite more Black people to the Shrine. I was fired up and filled with the Holy Spirit. Every week I brought about seventeen guests to church. Most of them were college students from Morehouse College and Clark College where I worked. I would stop and talk to the students on campus and would impress them about the things that I was learning at the Shrine. Some of them were totally unaware of the contributions that African people had contributed to the world. As a BTG group we brought at least 65 visitors to church each week. Black people near and far in large numbers came to join the Shrine on Sunday. There were many different groups in the church, all competing for membership and fundraising drives. After the drives we celebrated with glamorous dinner parties we called Cheza at the Shrine. It was moments like that that helped make the struggle so much more enjoyable. There were lots of members getting married in the Shrine. When my friend Mwalimu Mbiyu and Fundi Binta decided to get married he choose me to be his best man.

Once I completed basic training, I felt that the people in my group were my family. I had read the importance of group training in a book by the founder of the Shrine of the Black Madonna. He believed that the group provides an individual's salvation and that no one individual can wage a liberation struggle alone. He wrote, "Only a people who struggle together can carry on a revolution. As Black Christian Nationalists, we seek to free ourselves from individualism in order that we may become a people. The most important single aspect of both our faith and our program is the fact that we have rediscovered the process by which the individual can be led to divest himself of individualism and merge into the mystic, communal oneness of the Black nation."

I then moved up to advance leadership training and became a missionary for the church. I traveled to cities and towns in southern states where I had never been before standing in front of stores with a canister in my hand raising funds for the Shrine Missionary Outreach Program. These trips were adventures that I will never forget. I now understood better the changes that I had already made in my life since those days in Charleston.

I was becoming more disciplined than I had ever been before. I had found people who were willing to help me, and I was still learning so much at the Shrine that it was like attending a major university. At the Shrine I was fed spiritually, mentally, and physically. I felt the Shrine was my gift from God.

In January 1979, Cardinal Sondai Nyerere appointed me to a clerk's position in our Cultural Center and Bookstore. As far as I knew the Shrine's Cultural Center contained the largest collection of books written by Black people in North America. It was an honor to work there. I also felt that it was my intellectual duty to read as many of those books as I could in order to better serve our customers. These included *The Destruction of Black Civilization* by Chancellor Williams; *Introduction to African Civilization* by John G. Jackson; *The Blackman of the Nile and His Family* by Dr. Yosef Ben Jochannan; *World's Great Men of Color* by J.A. Rogers; and *The Black Man's Burden* by John Oliver Killens. The public schools in Charleston had taught me very little about slavery, the Black man's glorious history, and the Harlem Renaissance. If I had been taught more, I'm sure I would have been a better student. Now, with this new knowledge, I vowed to share it with anyone who would listen.

I was so devoted to the Shrine that I was soon drafted into the Holy Order of the Maccabees, the security force for the church. Under the leadership of my superior officers, I learned loyalty, commitment, and honor. In addition, I learned to march like a soldier, think like an armed officer, and protect my church like a lion.

I was also taught the importance of politics. Local, state and national elected officers create laws that can have positive or negative effects in our lives. In 1981, I worked with the Black Slate, the political arm of the Shrine, to help get former United Nations Ambassador Andrew Young elected as mayor of Atlanta, Georgia. On election day, I worked at the voting poll on

Martin Luther King, Jr. Drive near Vine Street. As I was standing in front of the station about 4:00 p.m., I noticed a young Black man and a middle-aged woman in a yellow and white dress getting out of a car. As they walked in my direction, I recognized them as Mrs. Coretta Scott King and her son, Martin Luther King, III. I greeted them and she returned the greeting. I offered them Black Slate flyers that I was handing out. She thanked me and said, "I have the Blue Slate, but I see we have some of the same candidates." Just before she entered the building, she turned around and smiled at me. "Wow!" I thought. "I just met Mrs. King herself!"

Earlier during my stay in Atlanta, I had met another famous person. At that time, I was working as a janitor at Emory University. One day I saw President Jimmy Carter walking down the hall after visiting his brother Billy who was a patient there. Several doctors and nurses' aides stepped aside to make room for Mr. Carter and his bodyguards. Everybody they passed greeted the former President respectfully and he in turn waved his hand and returned their greetings. As he came close, I felt a sense of awe that I was coming face to face with such a historic figure whom I had always admired and who had raised the minimum wage when he was in office. As the entourage got to where I was standing, I noticed that Mr. Carter was quite suntanned. He looked directly at me, and in response to my greeting, he said, "I'm doing fine. How about you?" followed by "Have a good day." Then he and his bodyguards got on the elevator and were soon out of sight.

CHAPTER 20

A Period of Change

My life had become so busy with my job and evening volunteer work for the Shrine that I hardly ever saw Annette in the apartment we shared. When two men I knew from the Shrine mentioned that they were looking for someone to rent the extra room in their three-bedroom apartment located only a few blocks from the Shrine, I felt that moving there would be less disruptive for my sister and save me time in transportation. After discussing the rent, I agreed to move in with them. When I got home, I told Annette about my decision. "Follow your heart," she said. "If it's more convenient for you, I'm all for it." She reminded me, though, that I would have to learn to cook for myself.

"That's no problem," I said. "The Shrine sells dinners to members in its dining hall, every day and I can eat there." After I told her that I would move at the end of the month, she kissed me on the cheek and wished me well. At the end of February 1979 one of my church brothers moved me in his truck to my new apartment. My two roommates were brothers, both security officers at the Shrine as I was.

Returning to my apartment one Sunday after church, I was surprised to see a very attractive young woman sitting alone in the living room reading a magazine. She introduced herself as Mawakana. I remembered seeing her at the service and thinking how beautiful she was. She said she was waiting for one of my roommates, Brother Osei, to come back and take her to lunch. While she waited she told me that she had only recently moved to Atlanta from Detroit. We had quite a nice conversation. She seemed intelligent as she commented on world events and how they affected Black people. I told her about the books I had read. I didn't realize how long we had been waiting, but I suddenly felt very hungry. Since neither of my roommates had come back, I invited her to go to dinner with me.

We left my apartment on Lucile Avenue across the street from the park and went to a wonderful Black-owned restaurant on Cascade Avenue called "The Beautiful Restaurant." The more she talked, the more convinced I was that she was the smartest woman I had ever met. She told me she was 24 years old and was a student at Georgia State University. I was twenty. She said she had a photographic memory. When dinner was over and I was walking her home, I asked her if I could see her again. We continued to date and eventually we became intimate. The more I saw of her, the more in love with her I became. She seemed as much in love with me as I was with her.

In August she went to Jamaica to visit friends. When she returned, she told me that she was pregnant. I was very happy and looked forward to getting married and being a father. However, during one of her visits to the doctor, he told her to bring me with her to her next appointment. When we went to his office together the following week, he informed us that the fetus was in her tube, a condition that was life threatening. He said that nothing could be done to save the fetus, and the best thing we could do was to have an abortion. I felt devastated. This was the second time a woman was not able to give birth to my child.

We continued to see each other, but after six months, the thrill of our relationship disappeared. We both knew that we were no longer in love and agreed to break up. We remained friends, however, and have kept in touch with one another throughout the years.

◆ ◆ ◆

After working for several years as a janitor, I felt that I needed to move on to a better job. Remaining a janitor was not my goal in life; I was destined for something better. And I needed to make enough money to at least support a family; I couldn't do that as a janitor. One of my friends, Seyoum, at the Shrine was a job consultant for a company in downtown Atlanta. I talked to him about my concerns. He got me a position at a meat packing company. My job was to help keep the freezer warehouse in order. The job paid ten dollars an hour, and I would be paid weekly. I was very happy to quit my janitor's job and advance to something better. My work hours were from 7 a.m. to 3 p.m. One day I saw a flier about an adult education program at a community center on Auburn Avenue near the Martin Luther King Center for Social Change. It was necessary during my training period at the Shrine to stop taking adult education classes, but now that I had finished my training, I was now free to continue my education. I took a bus to the center where one of the instructors gave me a tour. I signed up for reading, writing, and math classes. I enjoyed going to the center after work. I was getting really good in math.

After months on my new job, the meat company moved to a new location. Now I had to catch two buses in order to get to school. One day I asked my supervisor if I could work half a day and go to school the other half. He denied my request and instead suggested that I work the night shift, from 11 p.m. to 7 a.m. I did as he suggested. All the men on the night shift were much older than I was. They nicknamed me Baby Boy. My new job was to help unload the meat truck. I had to lift half sides of cows and heavy pig hides. This was much harder work than what I had done on the day shift, but I felt I could handle it and continued for months.

One night the union steward got upset with the workers and announced that he was resigning effective immediately. "Get yourselves a new leader," he said. "I'm tired of fighting management and none of you workers are supporting me."

At lunch time, the men began suggesting who should be the new leader, but each person they named declined to take on the extra responsibility. Then a voice from the back said, "I suggest Baby Boy. He's smart. Every time he goes on break he's reading a book." The others agreed, "Yes, Baby Boy would make a good union steward. I asked, "What would be my responsibilities?" One of the guys responded, "You have to go talk with management when things go wrong." The men laughed. Another man offered, "To keep our asses in check when we fuck up." There was more laughter. I asked if I would be making more money. The steward who had resigned said, "No, but the experience may be good for you." I agreed to take the job in spite of the fact that all the workers were Black and everyone in management was white. As we broke up to go back to work many of the workers came over to shake hands and promised to work with me.

At first everything went well. There were no problems between the union workers and management. As a leader, I made sure to get to work at least fifteen minutes before clock-in time. There were fifty men in the union, and I met with them once a week. Sometimes I had to stay after work to meet with managers.

As time went on, some of the union men began coming to work late and occasionally even drunk. Management got very upset with them and I had to intervene. At times union members became very disrespectful toward me and some even threatened to fight me. This began to make my job as steward especially difficult. In spite of my new title, I was still responsible for unloading the meat trucks. One night I felt a pain in my lower back after picking up too many sides of heavy beef. The pain got so bad that I was unable to work for several months and survived on workmen's compensation. Eventually, I had to be admitted to a hospital for back surgery. Doctors removed the L5 disc from my lower back.

The men often called my house to check on me and find out when I was coming back to work. They told me that I was a good union steward. Maybe I was, but I couldn't afford to continue doing the heavy lifting that I did before. In spite of the surgery, I still suffered pain which I assumed would be permanent. As a result, I sued the meat company and received a settlement. I knew I would have to find some other work that was not so physically challenging.

CHAPTER 21

Becoming a Poet

After my Workman's Compensation ran out, I still had the money from my law suit and a Pell grant, so I could afford to go back to school to learn a trade without the necessity of working at the same time. So, before I went home for Christmas, a white lady I knew from the Workman's Compensation office helped me enroll in Atlanta Area Technical College where I could study printing. I also had to study reading, English composition, and mathematics. My classes would begin in March.

One Tuesday night in 1983, the televised evening news reported that thousands of Ethiopian people were dying due to a major drought that had caused famine throughout their land. I was so deeply saddened by this news; I couldn't stop crying. Suddenly, from nowhere came the words of the first two poems I ever wrote; they were about the suffering of Black people. When my roommates Sefu, Kofi and Oladeinde came home later that night, I showed them the poems. Kofi read both poems aloud and liked them. Sefu and Oladeinde felt that this new creativity was certainly a gift from God and that I should work on developing my talent. When I arrived at school early the next morning, I went to my English teacher, Ms.

Dupree and showed her the poems. She edited them and said they were good. She encouraged me to show my poems to Ms. Christie Benton, whose class was just across the hall; Ms. Christie Benton taught typing. She liked the poems. She typed them up and attached them to the front wall for the other students to read. This was the first time I had written anything that attracted so much attention. It was a glorious moment for me, primarily because I had always believed that I was not smart and would never succeed at anything in school. The night I wrote those first two poems became one of the major turning points of my life. My new-found interest in poetry would boost my ego for the rest of my life. It was at that point that I knew I wanted to become a professional writer. I also knew that if I was going to become a poet, I needed to study the works of a few successful Black poets of different times like Paul Laurence Dunbar, Langston Hughes, Claude McKay, Gwendolyn Brooks, Naomi Long Madgett, Nikki Giovanni, Maya Angelou, and Haki R. Madhubuti.

My minister, Bishop Mbiyu Chui, also wrote poetry. Whenever I visited his apartment, we'd sit and critique each other's poems late into the night. Bishop Mbiyu, to me was one of the most talented brothers I had ever met. He wrote many of the plays for the Shrine and starred in them. He could sing and preach. He always encouraged people to believe in themselves. He kept my soul searching for what I wanted to become—a poet. I was living at the church residence hall on 66 Peeples Street and my roommate was Brother Adande. He admired my dedication to become a writer; he would take me to his job on the weekends to make copies of my poems. Sergeant Uwimana N. Olabisi, another good friend of mine in the Shrine, would always ask me to show her my poems in case they needed editing. She did a few corrections and told me to keep up the good work. She became like an older sister to me. When my family would come to Atlanta and visited me at the Shrine, Sergeant Uwimana treated them like they were her family. And my family loved her for that. I once took her to Charleston and walked her around town to see the sights for four hours. I am confident she will never forget that experience. She is now a permanent member of my family.

At Atlanta Area Technical School I was elected vice-president of my class. I was also recognized as the school poet. I became obsessed with poetry, often writing about four or five poems a day.

One day while riding the bus downtown from school, I heard a love poem in my head. I resisted the idea of writing it down, telling myself I was tired. But the next morning, a female student who had heard that I wrote poetry asked me to write a poem that she could give to her boyfriend. Everything she asked me to say I had heard in my head the day before. After that, I decided to always keep a pen or pencil and paper handy in case I was inspired. There were many inspirational and sorrowful moments in my life to write about.

While I was working at the Shrine's bookstore, I occasionally met Black authors who came for book signings. On one particular day, I walked inside and saw a flyer on the counter featuring John Oliver Killens. He was a Black author and one of the founders of the Harlem Writers Guild. His name fascinated me. The flyer said that on the following Tuesday he would be in Atlanta for a book signing at the West Hunter Branch Library on Martin Luther King, Jr. Drive. I knew I had to meet him. I asked Ewa, one of the female clerks, if we had any of his books. We did, and she walked me over to where a number of his books were. I learned that he was a fiction writer, playwright, essayist, and teacher. He had written such novels as *Young Blood* and *And Then We Heard the Thunder*, as well as a non-fiction book entitled *Black Man's Burden*. These books struck a nerve in me. I had just enough money to purchase *Young Blood*, a wonderful novel about ordinary

Black people in a small town in Georgia who were ready to die to obtain their rights.

I had not finished reading the book before that rainy Tuesday evening when John Oliver Killens and his wife Grace came to town. Earlier that day in school, I told many of my classmates about the author, inviting them to join me for his speech. However, not one other student came to the book signing, perhaps because it was raining too hard. I was so excited that rain could not keep me away. When I got on the bus from school, I forgot to ask the driver for a transfer that would allow me to take another bus to MLK Jr. Drive and the West Hunter Street Library, so I had to walk at least four miles in the rain to the library. Good thing I had my umbrella!

Once I arrived at the library, I was surprised to see so few people present. I didn't know what Mr. Killens looked like, so I didn't know which of those present might have been the author until the librarian introduced him. He was a brown-skinned elderly gentleman, quite short and soft-spoken. I did not expect such an ordinary looking man to present such a radical message. He didn't talk much about his books but concentrated on the problems in Black America. I could have sat for hours on end listening to him. Once he finished we applauded him heartily. The librarian stood and thanked us for coming out on such a rainy night to see the author. I felt blessed to be in John Oliver Killens' presence. When the librarian opened the floor for questions, I was the first to speak. "Mr. Killens," I asked, "what words of inspiration do you have for a young up-and-coming writer like me?"

He looked at me and said, "Good question, son. Get involved in any organization that is working for the uplift of Black people, and the struggle will teach you what to write about our people." My mind was ablaze because I knew that being a member of the Shrine of the Black Madonna was the best place for me to be. When the program was over, I walked over to him and gave him the Black man's handshake and brotherly hug. I told him I loved his name. I stayed for a small reception, then went home with my autographed copy of *Young Blood,* promising myself I'd read *Black Man's Burden.*

At school the next day, many of my classmates gathered around me to ask about the author's presentation. I told them that if they were that hungry for knowledge about the author they should never let another opportunity like that pass them by. I added that the author had made an everlasting impression on me and suggested that they go to the Shrine bookstore and buy his books.

Though my life was changing, I kept in touch with my family back in Charleston. I was sad to learn from my mother that Eddie had started drinking heavily and was now on medication. She also informed me that he had gotten into an altercation with a policeman and was sentenced to a year in prison. While there he suffered depression. When he was released I went home for Christmas to celebrate his homecoming. All the time I was there, we were inseparable. One day we went to Bogard Street to visit with our friends. Everyone was glad to see us. I had not seen them since high school. Some of them were still hanging out on the same corner where we used to gather and not doing much else. It was great seeing them again, but my life had changed. I was deeply involved with my church and we no longer had much in common. After a few hours I signaled Eddie that I was ready to go. We all hugged and told our friends goodbye.

As we were walking back home, Eddie told me that he had been hearing a man's voice in his head telling him to kill himself. He said that he was still taking his medication, but the voice continued to speak to him. I told him not to listen because sometimes our minds can play tricks on us, but he insisted that the voice was real. I was deeply disturbed by what he said. I couldn't imagine a world without Eddie in it. He had always been my best friend in all the world. Although we no longer lived in the same city, I missed him very much. He was constantly on my mind.

Before I left Charleston, I told my family about the problem Eddie had shared with me. They said he had mentioned the same thing to them many times. My mother had instructed Eddie's doctor to change his medication and had even arranged for him to see a psychiatrist.

I was told the day before my little sister Izetta's birthday, January 17, 1983, Eddie promised her a nice birthday present. But when the next morning came, he never mentioned the present at the breakfast table. He told Mama and Daddy how much he loved them and thanked them for all they had done for him. He left for work at Medical University Hospital where Clarissa also worked. Around 9:00 o'clock Eddie jumped from the seventh floor of the hospital, killing himself instantly.

I didn't learn what had happened until I got out of class that evening and went to church. One of the officers told me that my mother had called about an emergency and I needed to call home right away. When I called, Clarissa answered and told me the terrible news. I wanted to scream from the shock and pain I felt but tried to hold back my emotions until I got outside. I left church and started walking in the rain crying uncontrollably. My brother, my friend was gone. Never again would I see him alive and share with him intimate conversations we used to have about our concerns. I wrote some of my best poems during this period of grief.

I returned to Charleston for Eddie's funeral, then resumed my classes in Atlanta. His death left an empty place in my heart. For ten years I tried to hang a framed picture of Eddie on a wall in my apartment, but every time I looked at it, I felt so sad that I'd put it away in a drawer. I finally was able to accept the fact that he had lived his life the way he wanted to and I could concentrate on the fond memories of the times we spent together. Now his picture will always be prominently displayed on a wall wherever I may live.

Our lives went on. Eventually, my sister Annette moved back to Charleston to get married to Bobby, the love of her life. To this union were born three beautiful children, Stephanie, L.P., and Nicholas.

◆ ◆ ◆

Atlanta eventually became one of the top cities in America for crime. From 1979 to 1981 it received national attention due to the murders of 28 African American children, adolescents, and adults.

I recalled an incident that happened to me when I was still a student. As I walked home one Monday night, some Black guys pulled up in a gray station wagon. One of them pointed a gun at my face and demanded money. I told him I had no money and that I was a student. One of the other guys searched my pockets and found nothing but my driver's license, which he took. I was carrying an extra pair of blue jeans in my hand, along with some books. They took the jeans and the books, too. I was frightened to death. One of them said to the guy with the gun, "Shoot him." He looked at me for a moment and decided against it. Then they all got back in the car and drove off. I was never so relieved in my life. I ran home and told my three roommates what had happened to me, but I did not call the police then.

The following Friday, when I got off the bus near my house, I saw parked nearby what looked like the same station wagon of the guys who had robbed me. I walked behind the car and got the license plate number. Then I called the Atlanta Police Department and told them my story. They sent a white detective to take my report and the license plate number of the car. I thought for sure the thieves would be arrested. Instead, much to my surprise, a week later, two white male FBI officers cornered me in my front yard and arrested me for murdering a white female prostitute in an Alabama motel. I denied having anything to do with such a crime and had not been anywhere near the motel they mentioned. They pulled out a large photo of me as proof. I didn't know where they got it. When I told them I had gotten robbed two weeks earlier, they asked if I had any proof. "Yes," I said. "Let's go inside and I'll call the Atlanta Police Headquarters. They followed me and called the police. The officer they talked to confirmed that I had reported being robbed before the murder occurred, and the killer of the white prostitute had left my driver's license, that he had stolen from me, on her bed. That was enough to convince the FBI agent of my innocence. He called his office in Alabama and told the officer there that I was not the person who committed the murder. Over the speaker phone, I heard the agent in Alabama say, "Arrest that nigger anyhow. Somebody's gotta pay for this crime and it might as well be him." The agent with me responded, "We can't pin it on this guy; he's in school and doesn't have a record." Then he hung up the phone and said, "Son, it's a good thing you reported being robbed, because if you hadn't, you'd be going on a long ride to Alabama." We shook hands and he left.

♦ ♦ ♦

Just before I graduated from Atlanta Area Technical School with a certificate in printing and graphic arts, I set up a meeting with Cardinal Sondai (nicknamed "Son of Thunder") who had been promoted from bishop. He and I had developed a pretty good friendship over the years. I feel that he is the one who really inspired me to read books. Every time I would walk by his office he was reading and writing. I thought that he was the smartest man I had ever met. He once suggested that I read a book that cost $35.00. I said that was too much to pay for a book. He said, "Dadisi, don't ever put a price on knowledge if it's going to benefit you." I went out and bought the book. He told me that the Shrine had a printing shop in Detroit and if

I was interested, he would arrange for me to move there for more training. The idea of moving to Detroit, Michigan was exciting. I told him I certainly was interested. I knew that if I wanted to make something out of my life I had to leave Atlanta. Many of my church associates were beginning to feel that I was putting too much time and energy into my poetry and neglecting church business. I felt that I was destined to become a writer and writing required independent thinking, but it had nothing to do with being a member of the church.

I had a lot more personal growing to do and I knew God was not through with me yet. I simply needed to do some self-evaluation. Sometimes when you are trying to develop yourself and your associates don't understand your internal struggles, it may be best that you love them from a distance in order to find peace within your soul.

Over the years I enjoyed great group leaders in the church like Bishop Lindiwe, Sergeant Uwimana, Fundi Hawayna, Fundi Shakaru, Mwalimu Tarik, Fundi Djenaba, Fundi Zakiya , Bishop Ayanna, Cardinal Kimathi, Fundi Binta and Mwalimu Mbiyu, Lieutenant Karamoko, and a host of dedicated members at the Shrine in Atlanta. Some of them had become my best friends, but I felt it was time to move on. But those Atlanta years had been good for me. I had become aware of who I am and embraced my ancestral Swahili name presented to me by my team leader, Menjiwe.

With respect, I called my parents and got their permission to legally change my name from Marvin Leroy Alston to Dadisi Mwende Netifnet. I told them that I was not divorcing them, but that I simply wanted to change my name for religious reasons.

I had lived in Atlanta for eight great years. At the time of my departure, I was 26 years old. I had been dating Sister Tarasai, whom I loved. We had a beautiful relationship. It hurt me to leave her and my church family at

Shrine #9, but my goal to become a published poet and writer was very important to me and I felt I could accomplish it better in a different setting.

On the last Sunday in June 1986, Maccabees Kehinda, Corporal Adisa, Corporal Kokayi and Master Sergeant Mobutu arrived in Atlanta from Shrine #10 in Houston, Texas to drive me to Shrine #1 in Detroit where I would spend the next nine wonderful years of my life.

CHAPTER 22

Move to Motown

We arrived in Detroit at the Shrine's training center and residence hall at 700 Seward Avenue on Monday morning, June 30,1986. Included in the group were three other members from Houston that I had never met before. As I got out of the van, I looked up at the seven-story brick building that I would now call home. Several sisters and brothers who lived in the building came out to greet us. I knew General Chui from Atlanta. Mwalimu Irungu, Bishop Sala Adams, Bishop Malikh Clark and Fundi Ada, the sister who invited me out to the Shrine in Atlanta, Georgia also greeted us. She was happy to know that I was still active in the Shrine. Then we were escorted into the building's beautiful lobby. The first person we met inside was Mwalimu Kenyatta, the building manager. He welcomed us and gave us the keys to our apartments. A brother named Bobo escorted us to the elevator and to our apartments. When we got to Apartment 217 he told me, "This is yours." I entered and looked out the window in awe, realizing that now I was a resident of the city where the founder of Motown Records, Barry Gordy, produced and managed such vocalists as Mary Wells, Marvin Gaye, Smokey Robinson and the Miracles, The Temptations, The Jackson Five, Martha Reeves and the Vandells, Diana

Ross and the Supremes, Stevie Wonder, and The Four Tops and so many more. I hoped that someone would someday discover *me*. Though I didn't claim to be a singer, I believed that I could probably write some great songs that might become hits. After a while I went back down to the first floor to admire the beauty of the lobby with its cool red carpet, mahogany walls, and crystal chandelier. It all became even more clear to me the importance of the church's Missionary Outreach Program, the fundraising arm of the church. The money I was raising was helping to build highly respectable institutions for Black people.

Then I decided to visit the apartments of the other three new arrivals. I was surprised to find that theirs were much larger and better equipped than mine. Mine looked skimpy compared to theirs. I returned downstairs and asked Mwalimu Kenyatta if there was a larger apartment available. He said, "Yes, I forgot to tell you. Apartment 217 is just temporary. Your apartment 306 is being painted and will be ready for you to occupy next week." Satisfied, I went back up and stretched out on my bed, suddenly tired from the twelve-hour ride from Atlanta. I turned on the radio and happened to get a station that was playing the Temptations singing "Ain't Too Proud to Beg." I must have fallen asleep, because I was awakened by a phone call telling me it was time to come to dinner.

At dinner I learned from my assigned group leader Brother Kehinde & Tiombe that I was part of a team that would be going to Albany, New York later that evening to conduct Missionary Outreach for the church. We would return to Detroit on Friday morning, July 4[th.] Ours was one of about eight groups going to various states on Missionary Outreach assignments. I was impressed at how well the church's activities were organized, in both Atlanta and Detroit.

Later that evening, three officials, including Master Sergeant Mobutu, our team leader, and I loaded our assigned car in preparation for the journey. Mobutu mentioned that we would be going through Canada to cross over into New York. I became excited about going into a country I had only heard about.

When we got to the Ambassador Bridge leading to the city of Windsor, Ontario, I learned that we would be asked a few questions. We had to inform the border officials that we were from the U.S. passing through Canada to Albany, New York. I was instructed not to say anything more than I needed to say and let others do the talking. Being from Charleston, I had not yet lost my strong Geechee accent. Geechee, is a creole language spoken by the Gullah people who live in the coastal regions of South Carolina, Georgia and northeast Florida. The group thought that my accent might cause some suspicion. The line of cars was very long. Some of those ahead of us were being pulled over to the side by the Canadian authorities. I began to feel nervous. When we finally got to the front of the line, the inspector asked each of us our citizenship. I responded "U.S" as clearly as I could. Then he asked how long we would be in Canada and Mobutu, answered, "We're just passing through on our way to Albany, New York." When asked, he also assured the official that we were not bringing any alcohol, tobacco, or weapons into Canada. We were then given permission to continue and I breathed a sigh of relief. I wasn't too sure that Canada was the right place for me.

However, as we passed through Windsor and many other cities, I began to fall in love with the country. I noticed that each city was very clean. What *really* blew my mind was seeing Niagara Falls late that night. We parked the car and ran toward the sound of rushing water. When we reached the tourist building we saw the rainbow-colored lights shining on the falling waters. The scene was breathtaking and beautiful. It was a magical moment for me. There we were, looking at one of the wonders of the world. I felt blessed to see such a magnificent sight. The mist coated my face like morning dew. I could have stayed there forever, but I knew we had to move on. Two people slept while the driver and the person in the front passenger seat stayed awake. We alternated when the first team became tired.

We arrived in Albany at about 5:00 a.m. After checking into a Red Roof Inn to change clothes, we went out for breakfast. Two hours later, the team dropped me off in front of a Kmart store where I would raise funds for the Missionary Outreach Program for the rest of the day. Albany, the capital of New York, was nothing like New York City. I saw no vendors on the streets selling things, nor did I see tall buildings or prostitutes walking up and down the street as I had on New York's 42nd Street. I would have enjoyed sightseeing but I didn't have transportation to see much of anything else. Furthermore, this was not a pleasure trip; it was strictly church business. The team picked me up from Kmart twelve hours later. The other missionaries and I went to dinner, using the stipend provided by the church. Afterwards we returned to the hotel to rest. We would perform the same routine for the next three days. Then we were picked up from our assigned spots and driven back through Canada to Detroit without incident at the border.

We arrived at the National Training Center around 5:00 a.m. the next day. The Maccabees on duty greeted us in the lobby. We unloaded our personal belongings from the car and turned over the money we had collected to the Missionary Outreach Office. Finally, we retired to our apartments to rest.

When I woke up the next morning, I showered and headed downstairs for breakfast. In the dining hall, members were sitting at various tables, talking and eating. I entered the serving line, placed my breakfast on a tray and then joined some members at a table with an empty chair. Among those seated were Bishop Nilaja, who headed the Shrine national office in Detroit, her mother, Fundi Amina, her sister Fundi Tene, and Bishop Tunu, whom I learned later was from Spartanburg, South Carolina. I was also introduced to Mwalimu Diallo whom I was told I would be working with. "I've been looking forward to meeting you," he said. "Welcome to Detroit." I told him I also was looking forward to training with him at the printing press at Shrine #4. "We'll relax today," he said. "Tomorrow morning I'll take you on a tour of Shrine #4."

After a few pleasantries, I excused myself and went back to my apartment. I received a phone call later that morning telling me that I had been reassigned to Bishop Olubayo's group, that several church members were going to Belle Isle for a picnic around one o'clock, and that I was welcome to join them. I thanked him and said I'd love to go. I still had time to relax for a couple of hours. The name "Belle Isle" rang a bell. I remembered that this was where the famous race riot started on June 20, 1943. The violence between Blacks and whites spread to Detroit and continued for several days. I remembered reading that it was the deadliest riot in American history. I thought it would be interesting to see this historic island.

Wearing a short-pants outfit, I went down to the lobby at 12:50. There were still many members I had not yet met. Of those who introduced themselves was Bishop Olubayo, my new group leader. A middle-aged woman who spoke with a strong Jamaican accent. At her request I followed her to the vestibule where about fifteen brothers and sisters were congregated. After getting their attention, she introduced me. They greeted me warmly. Then we all got into the church vans and headed for the park.

For over the next two and a half years this would be one of the best groups I had been a part of. We performed many great works for the church and Bishop Olubayo proved to be a wonderful and effective group leader. As a group on Sunday evening we would sometimes go to movies, jazz concerts or retreats. In the liberation struggle we took time out to have fun.

When Saturday morning arrived, I received a call to go downstairs to the dining hall for breakfast. There I met Mwalimu Diallo. After that, he took me to Shrine #4 where the printing shop was located. "Leisure time is over," he said. "It's now time to go to work. You need to learn how to operate every machine we have. It will take some time and patience, but I know you're up to it."

"I'm eager to learn all I can," I replied.

On our way to the east side, Diallo told me that he had gone to school to learn both printing and graphic arts and had been working at the print shop for many years. Soon we arrived at a small white brick building that had no windows. We entered from the back. When he turned on the lights I observed a big room containing several machines. One was a Heidelberg press; another was a binding press for smaller jobs. On a metal table I noticed a number of church flyers, evidently from a completed job. I told him that my only experience had been on an AB Dick small press.

"Don't worry, I'll teach you to operate every machine we have." He beckoned me to follow him to a back room that was completely dark. When Diallo turned on red lights I could see a number of shelves that held all kinds of bottles, each containing chemicals. There were six empty trays on a table that Diallo said he used to develop the films. We left the room and I had to readjust my eyes from the dark.

I followed Diallo to another section of the building where there was a machine for burning the plate to put on the printing press. We went to the front of the building. The first room was quite large with several screened white T-shirts with "Alkebu-lan Academy" printed on them. Diallo said that he laid out the T-shirts in this area to allow them to dry. Another room appeared to be an office equipped with four desks and a lot of tables on which a lot of photos were spread out. I went over to look at them. Some showed various Detroit church events while others depicted the Shrine's three national regions. Diallo invited me to have a seat at one of the desks and told me that organizing these photos would be my first assignment. He handed me some large photo binders and note pads. Then he pointed out a large bookshelf with many more Black photo binders containing numerous pictures. The pictures and negatives had to be matched with the year and month each photo was taken. Before I knew it, I realized that we had been working for eight hours. Day after day we worked together as Diallo shared his expertise. For the next nine years, I became quite knowledgeable in the art of printing.

A month after I was in Detroit, the Shrine political arm "The Black Slate," organized busloads of members and supporters to ride up to the Michigan Capital building in Lansing, Michigan to protest South African apartheid and for the release of Nelson Mandela. We were greeted by a member of the Shrine who was a Michigan State House Representative Carolyn Cheeks Kilpatrick. We called her Fundi Nataki.

She escorted us upstairs to the Capital building. She had the Speaker of the House acknowledge our presence in the balcony. The lawyers downstairs were voting on whether Michigan should divest in South Africa. As the lawyers were voting we walked outside of the building in front of the Capital demanding that Michigan divest in South Africa apartheid. Our demand with the support of many others encouraged Michigan lawyer to divest in South Africa. We were so happy and in 1990 President FW de Klerk released Nelson Mandela from prison after serving 27 years.

During my stay in Detroit, my time was divided among many of the groups of the church. One group that I was extremely honored to be a part of was the Holy Order of the Maccabees. This group was the security force for the church. When I first arrived in Detroit I was one of about fifteen Maccabee cadets. We reported for physical training with Major Kokayi at 5:00 a.m. Monday through Wednesday. It was important to be on time.

If anyone was late, Major Kokayi would order the entire group to do at least fifty push-ups. No one really liked that because sometimes we were outside in the freezing cold. We'd go inside to the training center's Hall of Pentecost, a room the size of a small gym, and learn the basics of martial arts. Being a part of the Maccabees helped me to become more security-conscious. We were taught to be aware of the enemy within as well as the enemy without. Our church was working to build institutional power for Black people. We learned that power is not given; it is earned, and that we needed to protect it.

During our training Major Kokayi made sure that we enjoyed great fellowship. On Sunday nights, my group members would often come to my apartment with lots of food and drink. We'd play cards, dance, or just listen to jazz, sometimes staying and enjoying each other's company far into the night. I now have at least 500 albums, most of which I bought used. Over the years I rose from cadet to the position of lieutenant.

Often as a security officer, I would escort Jaramogi Abebe Agyeman (Rev. Albert B. Cleage, Jr.), the founder of the Shrine of the Black Madonna, to his apartment, or wherever he wanted to go. It was an honor to be with this man of vision. I would ask him questions about how he started the church and the direction he wanted the church to go. I also thanked him for establishing the Shrine because it was there that I learned about the science of Kua, which involved meditation, yoga, and Tai Chi, and promoted the macrobiotic diet. During the winter I would sometimes watch football games with him at his apartment. He always made me feel welcome.

I had read and enjoyed his poems that were available in the church's bookstores. I told him that I was writing poetry too and hoped to get my poems published someday. In addition to Jaramogi I also got along well with his sister, Cardinal Nandi, who established and became the national director of the Shrine of the Black Madonna Cultural Centers and Bookstores. I often drove her around town when she wanted to go shopping. Sometimes she showed her appreciation by buying me a piece of clothing or something to help me decorate my apartment. She also gave me books that publishers had sent to her for review. She listened intently to my dream of becoming a writer and encouraged me. She made a very positive impact in my life.

◆◆◆

Being a traveling missionary for my church for seventeen years was an adventure. Since childhood I had always wanted to travel and see as much of the world as I could. Raising funds for the expansion of the various Shrines took me to over thirty states including Florida, Massachusett and Wisconsin to name only a few. I had the privilege of viewing beautiful landscapes, experiencing the blistering heat of summer, marveling at the rainbow-colored leaves of autumn, and shivering in the freezing snow of winter. But riding in a car for so many hours eventually took its toll on my already injured lower back. I realized that I would have to inform the Bishops' Council that I would have to discontinue my traveling. Now as a full-time Missionary I realized that all my various duties over the years had been labors of love.

CHAPTER 23

A Dream Comes True

had been in Detroit for about five years when I visited the main public library and saw a stack of flyers near the entrance. I picked up a copy and saw that it was an announcement of a self-publishing workshop sponsored by Lotus Press, Inc. Those who wished to attend were required to submit three original unpublished poems to the address provided. Only five to ten applicants would be selected. I was so excited that I forgot what I went to the library for and immediately turned around and left, running all the way back to my apartment at the BCN National Training Center. I pulled down from a shelf a collection of about a hundred poems that I had written but had never tried to get published. I quickly decided which three poems I would submit. I took them downstairs and asked two of my most literary friends, Fundi Amina and Sergeant Tsehynesh to proofread them. I went back to my apartment and addressed an envelope to Dr. Naomi Long Madgett, as instructed, found a stamp and deposited the poems in the nearest mailbox with a quick prayer that they would meet with her favor. I had heard of Dr. Madgett and the work she was doing as founder, publisher and editor of Lotus Press but had never met her. Two weeks later, I received a reply from her congratulating me and informing me of my selection to attend the workshop. She provided the address and location of the workshop and instructed me to be there the following Tuesday at 6:00 p.m. I was so elated that I could not control my tears.

The following Tuesday evening a friend drove me to a house on Santa Barbara Drive. (I was expecting the workshop to be in an office, but I later learned that Dr. Madgett was using this house as the office for Lotus Press but was living with her husband at another residence about five minutes away. I rang the bell and was greeted by Dr. Madgett herself. I introduced myself and she invited me into the living room saying, "I enjoyed reading your poems. I think you have great potential." There were two other people already seated; we introduced ourselves and chatted as we waited for the others to arrive. Dr. Madgett informed us that six people had been selected to participate in the workshop. One of whom was Hilda Vest who, with her husband Donald, had just recently taken over the ownership of Broadside Press founded by Dudley Randall, the oldest Black publishing company specializing in poetry in the country. I felt proud to be one of the chosen few.

After the others arrived, we talked for a few minutes. Then Dr. Madgett took over and explained how we would begin. She provided us with paper and pens and advised us to take notes. Each person would read his or her three poems. Then the group would critique each poem and make helpful suggestions on how it could be improved. Finally, Dr. Madgett would offer advice. From these discussions, I learned a great deal about imagery, rhyme, and meter that I didn't know. I had been under the impression that poetry had to rhyme and make sense and little else. I learned also about the difference between traditional rhymed verse, free verse, and blank verse. She read examples of each form. The next activity would be for each person to revise his/her poems based on the discussions. We would meet each Tuesday and Thursday at the same time and place for as long as necessary, probably at least six weeks. However, our leader encouraged us to call her at any time if we needed help. She also recommended that we revise other poems we'd written based on what we had learned. Most of us had enough poems to publish a book.

As the session continued, we were encouraged to call her by her first name. It took me several visits to feel comfortable calling her Naomi because I had so much respect for her. Eventually, I visited her home to see if she needed me to do chores. There was nothing I wouldn't do for her. On the days when we had workshops I was the first to arrive and the last to leave. I felt that she held the key to my success as a writer and would lead me in the right direction. I considered her my literary mother, and it wasn't long before I started calling her Mother.

The next phase of our workshops included learning how to lay out a typed book-length manuscript and get it camera-ready for the printer. She set up card tables on which we could work. Numbering the pages correctly was a challenge, as well as knowing which pages should not show the page number although they were numbered. She taught us how to make a "dummy" (a collection of letter-size blank pages), fold the pages in half, and number the pages. When we separated these pages, we could see that they were not in consecutive order. For instance, page 1, faced page 26 instead of following page 2. In this way we could avoid a serious error. After we learned how to layout our books and Mother checked them for accuracy, we were ready to take our material to a printer.

She gave me the name and address of a printer in Southfield that I could pay to print, staple, and trim my book. Within a few days I went to the printer and a young white lady greeted me. I showed her my manuscript and asked her how much it would cost to print my 100-page manuscript. She thumbed through the pages and said, "You did a great job with the layout." Then she added, "The cost will depend on how many copies you want and the quality of the paper. If you want 100 copies on the best paper, the cost will be $900". I was shocked. I had no idea it would cost so much. I took the manuscript, thanked her, and left.

I had very little money. For the last five years my church had provided me with all my necessities. Deeply disappointed, I went straight to Mother's house to tell her the bad news. "Let me think," she said. "This is a good manuscript. There may be other possibilities." She went into another room and came back with some papers. After shuffling through them for a few minutes, she said, "James W. Peeples, a Black man owns "The Winston-Derek Publishing Company in Nashville, Tennessee. Write him a query letter, along with copies of about five of your best poems and ask him if he would consider publishing your book." Then she added, "Be sure to include a stamped, self-addressed envelope with enough postage for their return."

I wrote the letter right away and she checked it for errors. The next day I typed it and mailed it with the poems and the return envelope. Less than two weeks later, I received a response asking me to send the entire manuscript for consideration. One month later I received a contract to publish *Poetry for Today's Young Black Revolutionary Minds*. And I didn't have to pay any money in advance! I was ecstatic! Immediately I took the contract to Mother's house because I wanted to be sure I understood it. She assured me that it was genuine. I hugged her tightly. I think she was as happy as I was. I offered a silent prayer thanking her for her help and praising God who had made this dream a reality.

It was a Thursday morning in February, 1993 when the mailman delivered something very special. I was in the lobby of the National Training Center when the front desk called me to get a box addressed to me. When I opened it, it contained two copies of my very own book with a glossy green and black cover. "Thank you, Lord!" I shouted. "Thank you, my good

Lord!" I shouted so loud that the three other people in the lobby heard me and rushed over to see what I was so happy about. It was with great pride that I showed them one of my books and announced, "This is my own book of poems. I just received it from my publisher." I called Mother Naomi to tell her the good news, but she was out of town. I mailed one of the books to my parents in Charleston and read the other copy over and over in disbelief.

The following week I received an invitation to a dinner party as the guest of a friend. I was surprised and happy to see Mother Naomi and her husband, Leonard Andrews, already seated. I greeted them warmly and told them about my new book. "Wonderful!" she said, kissing me on the cheek. "When can I see it?" I told her I had a copy in the car and ran outside to get it. She handled it as if it was gold. "Is this my copy?" she asked. I explained that this was my only copy but that she would be the first to get a copy as soon as I ordered some. The following week I received more copies and was happy to give her the first one.

I took other copies to *The Detroit News*, *The Michigan Chronicle* and *The Detroit City View*. All three newspapers published feature stories about my book and me. I felt blessed by the support of the media. I later received calls from local radio and television stations inviting me to come in for broadcast interviews. I was even on the six o'clock news. The story of my journey from illiteracy to published poet and author was an example that inspired others that goals are achievable with a positive attitude, determination, and hard work.

CHAPTER 24

Mother Africa

One snowy Monday morning in February, 1994 Lieutenant Adisa and I were talking and half listening to the radio as we drove to the Chrysler dealership to pick up one of the church's new cars. Suddenly we stopped talking as we heard the words, "Adventure to the Homeland." Listening carefully, we learned that McDonald's restaurant and Mix 92.3 Radio were sponsoring a contest for a 10-day, all-expense paid trip for two to West Africa. Did we hear correctly? We were completely silent as we listened for more details. This trip was in observation of Black History Month and in honor of Alex Haley, author of the famous book, *Roots*, who had died the year before. The trip included Senegal and Gambia, home of Kunta Kente, the main character in Mr. Haley's book. Adisa and I were equally excited when we learned that all we had to do to enter this contest was to register at any McDonald's restaurant.

After Adisa and I retrieved the car from the dealership, he drove the new car home and I followed in the one we came in. He said he was going to stop at a McDonald's on the way home to register for the trip.

"Great," I said. "I want to register, too." In just a few blocks he saw a McDonald's and pulled into the parking lot. I was right behind him. Once inside, he ordered a cup of coffee while I filled out five copies of the short entry form since there was no limit on how many forms one could submit. He filled out five forms, too. I really wanted to win that contest. I could think of nothing else.

After we got back, I went to as many restaurants as I could find. I knew that, if I wanted to win, I would have to fill out a lot of the registration forms and mail them as instructed to Radio Station Mix 92.3. Every day during that month, I visited as many McDonalds as I could, finally covering each one in Detroit. I must have mailed at least 200 entry forms. As far as I knew, only my girlfriend Zakiya had mailed as many as I had. We made an agreement that if either of us won, we would invite the other along for the trip. We also agreed to split the one thousand dollars allotted for spending money.

At long last, Mix 92.3 Radio would be announcing the contest winner on Monday morning. Zakiya and I had prayed about it the night before while I was at her house. Before I went home, I kissed her, and we wished each other the best.

About seven o'clock Monday morning the telephone rang and awakened me. I was afraid to answer it, but the calls kept coming so I finally answered. Captain Cheo had been calling me. He sounded excited. "You won the trip to West Africa!"

I didn't believe him. "Don't play with me," I said. "You know how much I wanted to win."

"I ain't lying. There's a lot of people waiting for you in the lobby to congratulate you." I was still sleepy and didn't know whether to believe him or not, but reluctantly I dressed and went downstairs to the lobby, hoping the message was true.

Lieutenant Adisa and several of our church members were already in the lobby. They hugged me and congratulated me. Right then, I heard the radio announcer. "The winner of McDonald's contest is Dadisi Netifnet. Mr. Netifnet, please call the station to claim your trip to West Africa." Only then did the whole thing sound real. Everybody in the lobby began to chant my name, "Dadisi! Dadisi! Dadisi!"

I called the number the radio announcer gave. I identified myself and the person on the end said, "You don't sound surprised. Are you?"

I explained, "I was sleeping when I got the call and thought I was dreaming."

He assured me that it was not a dream. "You and your guest will indeed be going to West Africa."

The reality finally sunk in; I whispered, "Thank you, Lord."

My girlfriend Zakiya had heard the news on the radio and called in great excitement. "Am I still going to be your guest?"

"Of course," I responded. I'm a man of my word." As promised, we would split the $1,000.00 I would get for expenses between us.

There was so much to do that we did not leave for Africa until July. In preparation we had to fill out a lot of papers, take dozens of shots to keep us healthy, and wait weeks for our passports. Eventually we were ready for our ten day visit to Senegal and Gambia. We spent our last night in Detroit at a hotel near Metro Airport. We got up early the next morning and boarded the plane to New York City where we would meet a representative of McDonald's restaurants.

As we were leaving JFK International Airport, a man holding a large sign that read: "Winners of Adventure to the Motherland" greeted us. After checking our identification, he loaded our luggage into a long black limousine. Weaving easily through traffic, he drove us to downtown Manhattan to a beautiful French hotel where we would spend the night. Entering the hotel at least fifty other contest winners from all over the United States greeted us. Except for two or three couples, all of them were Black. The coordinator of the "Adventure to the Motherland" project was Bill Haley, son of the highly regarded historian, Alex Haley.

The hotel staff escorted us to a Presidential suite on one of the higher floors where we would have breakfast before retreating to our separate rooms. The large room was filled with people and all kinds of delicious food. Bill Haley and other McDonald representatives joined us. Finally, a woman began giving all the winners keys to our rooms. Since we would not leave for Africa until the next morning, we had a free day. Zakiya and I went sightseeing around Time Square and Broadway. As instructed, we all met in the lobby at 5:00 p.m. to board the bus for a reception at the Arthur Schomburg Research Center in Harlem that documents the history, life, and culture of Black people the world over. I was aware of the wealth of information collected by Mr. Schomburg, a Black man from Jamaica, during the 1920s, and its ongoing additions by various scholars, so I was elated to be going to this important Harlem center bearing his name.

After we stepped off the bus and entered the building, I was filled with awe to see the many exhibits about the history of Black people. I was aware that there was much more information that was not readily visible in this building. Two of Zakiya's girlfriends who lived near New York met us at the reception to wish us a safe trip. Zakiya and I took two sets of pictures with McDonald's sponsors, Bill Haley, and the Ambassador of Gambia. The Ambassador delighted us with a slide presentation of Gambia.

After the reception, most of the group boarded the three buses back to the hotel, but Zakiya and I decided to check out the night life in downtown Manhattan instead. We found out that this area was true to its reputation.

The next morning, we boarded the Air Afrique plane for Senegal. I was astounded to see that the entire flight crew was Black. I couldn't resist shaking hands with all of them. As we soared across the Atlantic Ocean the sky darkened, but before long it was already morning and the sun was shining again even though it was still night in the USA. Hours later, we landed and went through customs. After claiming our luggage, we went outside and got on the buses that were waiting for us. I was rejuvenated to see the thousands of African people probably on their way to work.

We soon arrived at our hotel and checked into our rooms. Zakiya and I left our luggage there and at once went to the dining room for breakfast where we met some of the Senegalese dignitaries. We ate a hearty breakfast, washing it down with some red juice that was unfamiliar. By the time we returned to our room, I had begun to feel sick and rushed to the bathroom with a bad case of diarrhea. I felt embarrassed to be so sick in Zakiya's presence, but as soon as I came out, Zakiya rushed in with the same problem. We realized that our system was unfamiliar with the food. After each meal, we raced each other to the bathroom. Eventually I guess our stomachs settled down and adjusted to the food.

I spent my ten days in Senegal and Gambia from June 28 to July 9, 1994, soul-searching, trying to make sense of my life as an American and my African heritage. I met many African brothers and sisters who embraced us enthusiastically as their "gone away brother and sister." My heart rejoiced at their greetings, "Welcome home, my brother!" I felt they were sincere about our kinship. It warmed my heart to visit hundreds of villages in these two West African countries. I bought many authentic African artifacts and traded others with the brothers and sisters I met.

Much of the landscape was breathtaking. Have you ever seen a pink lake? Pink Lake in Senegal is believed to be the only lake in the world that reflects a pink radiance. I walked in it. I bathed in it. I meditated in it. I could have stayed there forever. From there we went to the shore of the Atlantic Ocean and enjoyed playing in the water. It was there that I saw the spectacle of a man calmly walking the waters in a rough current. He came from so far out that at first, he was only visible as a speck on the horizon. As he came closer, he became more visible. One female tourist turned to me and asked, "Who is that?"

I simply replied, "Jesus." When he finally reached shore, we could see that he was an African surfer, but the smoothness with which he negotiated the water and the range of his feat convinced me to stick with my original answer.

One of the most memorable events of this trip was a visit to Gambia—the village of the ancestors of Kunta Kente of Alex Haley's *Roots*. There were three busloads of tourists that went to the village that day. Village people, wearing their traditional clothing, came out to greet us. They were dancing and singing as if they were as glad to see us as we were to see them. We were told that the drum playing announced our arrival and that accompanying our festivities was only for special occasions.

I was so engrossed in the activities that I got on the bus without signing the permanent visitors' registry. However, I did leave with one of the elders a copy of my book, *Poetry for Today's Young Black Revolutionary Minds.*

The main highlight for me in Senegal was our visit to Gorée Island, just off the coast of Dakar. I was one of about a hundred tourists and native Africans who took a ferry boat to the island. Gorée Island was the main holding station where captured slaves were held before being transported to the western world. During our short journey, several young African men jumped off the boat into the Atlantic Ocean, swimming alongside us toward the island. When we arrived hundreds of children greeted us shouting, "My brothers, my sisters." They escorted us to the slave house in a parade. Once inside, there was complete silence. I'm sure that all the visitors felt the same extreme pain as I did as we imagined what our ancestors must have suffered in this awful prison while they waited to be packed on a ship like sardines for the Middle Passage. The curator of what is now a museum displayed many artifacts that were tools of the system of slavery. I still have painful memories of a small door known as "The Door of No Return." Through this one-way door a hundred million slaves passed to begin their journey away from the motherland forever. Actually, I felt my soul was out there moving through the water.

On the last day of this incredible journey, Bill Haley asked me to recite one of my poems. It was "I Shall Never Forget Mother Africa" which I had written just a few days before.

Back in the United States, all my friends asked me a myriad of question about my trip. In addition, I was asked to write an article that was published in *The Detroit Free Press*. Even an elderly gentleman who had been to Africa fourteen times himself questioned me for details. I wondered what he thought I had experienced in my only trip that he had missed on his many, but I finally realized that no two people visiting the same places come away with the same impressions. Even now, many people who have never been to Africa ask me to share with them my experiences in the Motherland. I am always happy to oblige.

I pray that my good fortune will someday take me back again to my ancestors' original home. God bless Mother Africa!

CHAPTER 25

Way Down in Egypt Land

One evening in March 1995, when I entered the Shrine of the Black Madonna Cultural Center and Bookstore in Detroit, I noticed a stack of flyers on the counter. Always curious, I picked one up to see what it was about. It was an announcement of a two-week trip to Egypt. Although I had visited two other countries in Africa just the year before, I knew I had to go. Immediately, I got on the security phone and called the number listed on the flyer to get more details. The trip included two meals a day and daily study of the history of ancient Black Egyptians. I had already studied a great deal of the history in classes taught at the Shrine. I still had in my notebooks several of the many quotations cited below:

Cheikh Anta Diop wrote, "Egypt is to Africa and African people as Greece is to Europe and European people."

Brian Brown wrote in *The Wisdom of the Egyptians*, "Egypt has been called the 'Father of History and the Mother of Civilization" and well may be called both, for her influence upon the ancient world has been great.

"A race of men now rejected for their Black skin and wooly hair founded the study of the laws of nature, those civil and religious systems which still govern the universe," wrote Count C.F. Volney in *Ruins of Empire*.

Indus Khamit Kush wrote, "Four thousand years before the Christian era we find that Egypt had a school of architecture and sculpture, a recorded literature, religious ceremonies, mathematics, astronomy, and music when the inhabitants of Europe were dwelling in caves and ages before the race of Hebrews became a nation."

And finally, "We conclude, therefore," wrote Dr. W.E.B. Du Bois in *The World and Africa*, "that the Egyptians were Negroid and . . . believed themselves descended . . . from the Black people of the South."

The man on the telephone invited me to come to his home on Boston Boulevard for more details. The house was close to where I was staying so it was easy for me to find. When I rang the doorbell, a tall Black man greeted me and welcomed me into his beautiful, spacious home. He introduced me to another elderly gentleman when I entered the living room. The three of us sat down and had a very pleasant conversation. Eventually we got into the details of the trip. I found that the trip would take place in August 1995 and would cost $1,200, which could be paid in installments. All the money would have to be paid by July 1. Before I left, I made a deposit of one hundred dollars, and every Tuesday evening after that, I would pay another installment until paid in full.

At each visit, I would learn more about Egyptian history. These gentlemen had visited that country more than a dozen times and were very knowledgeable about the Black presence in ancient Egypt. They showed me many pictures and told me a great deal about some of the kings and queens.

I also talked to the ministers at the Shrine and went to the library as often as I could. As I anticipated the trip I became more and more excited. I could hardly wait for August to come.

◆ ◆ ◆

In the meantime, the Shrine Church had a three-day conference in Houston, Texas in July. I decided to attend with others who were going from Detroit. This was my second visit to Houston. I went to many sessions and renewed friendships with some people I knew and made many new friends. But all that was overshadowed by what happened on the last night. At the party in Fellowship Hall I noticed a beautiful young lady whom I had never seen before. I introduced myself to her and learned that her name was Kharisma. I found her very easy to talk to. During our conversation I learned that she was not married and that she had two little sons, but they were out of town visiting their father. I found myself mysteriously drawn to her and stayed with her for the rest of the evening dancing, talking, and laughing. Around midnight when activities were winding down, we stayed and helped clean up Fellowship Hall. Instead of going our separate ways, she invited me to her house to continue our conversation, promising to take me back to the hotel. Instead, I ended up spending the night on her living room couch. I was due to leave Houston the next morning. After breakfast we hugged and kissed goodbye, promising to keep in touch. My girlfriend Zakiya and I had broken up and I couldn't get Kharisma off my mind. After I got back to Detroit, she was all I could think about. But my trip to Egypt was close at hand, and I knew I had to shift gears mentally.

It was a hot Saturday morning in August when Captain Cheo dropped me off at the house on Boston Boulevard to board a bus already filled with Black people of all ages who were also traveling to Egypt. The bus took us from Detroit to Toronto, Canada. We flew from there to JFK Airport in

New York where we boarded Air Egypt after clearing customs. The crew members were all very light skinned Muslims. The flight to Egypt would take fourteen hours with no planned stops for fuel, which was a surprise for me. A schoolteacher sat next to me. She told me she had to see Egypt before she died. I responded that this would be another important period of enlightenment for me.

We arrived in Cairo around 3 p.m. the following day. When we deplaned, unbearable heat struck us. It must have been a hundred degrees. A truckload of heavily armed soldiers met us on the runway. I wondered if there was a threat of terrorism, but I later learned that they were there to protect us from any danger that might occur. Arabic Muslims from the Middle East controlled this part of Africa. They had conquered Northern Africa around the seventh century.

Once we got off the airplane and cleared customs, we boarded a bus to our hotel. On our way, we stopped and paid homage to the late President Anwar Sadat, the last Black pharaoh to rule Egypt. Large marble columns with lotus flowers at the top surrounded his burial site. The burial site is located across the street from where he was assassinated on October 6, 1981 by Muslim extremists during a military parade. We all gathered around the burial site while the sponsor of the trip said a prayer; then we boarded the bus again. I wondered why there were so many people on the streets. Our tour guide explained that Cairo was so over populated that some of the homeless people lived in the cemetery. We saw some dark-skinned people, but many of the people we saw had light skin; I assumed they were from the Middle East.

We soon arrived at a beautiful five-star hotel. The first thing I saw as I got off the bus was the Great Pyramid of Giza. The sun was setting and its golden glow enhanced the magnificence of the pyramid. It appeared to be near to the hotel, but it was actually far away.

After we checked into the hotel and deposited our luggage in our rooms, we were directed to a large room where a welcoming committee greeted us. Afterward we ate dinner as a group. After that we were free to do whatever we wanted. I took this opportunity to relax and reflect on the reality of being in this ancient, historic land.

Every morning before it got too hot, we had a different experience. They included riding camels around the three pyramids, riding a boat down the Nile, and visiting the Valley of the Kings where we saw the tomb of King Tutankhamen; it included all the items he was believed to need in the afterlife. We also visited Luxor, where the great universities were, and the temple of Queen Hatshepsut, the only Black Egyptian female pharaoh. Then we went to Memphis, the capital of the oldest kingdom in the ancient world. We also visited the world-famous Museum of Antiquities in Cairo, where some of the remarkably well-preserved relics were six thousand years old. We saw the mummies of Black pharaohs with their wooly hair. We also visited Abu Simbel where we saw the two massive rock temples, as well as the 3,000-year-old monument to Rameses II. What an amazing experience!

Every night after dinner we discussed what we had seen and learned that day. Every tour guide informed us that it was Black Africans who founded Egyptian civilization and ruled Upper and Lower Egypt for thousands of years. In later years, the rulers were Greek, then Roman, and later Muslims.

The white Arabic store owners or managers with whom we came in contact were very kind. They offered us free soft drinks or bottles of water. In the evening when some of us went out shopping, we would often see Black Egyptians who would greet us with such words as "Welcome home, brother," just as they did in West Africa.

Not all my questions about the Black presence in Egypt were answered, but I was determined to continue my research back in the United States. On our last full day, I got up early. Since we would not be leaving until evening, we had some free time. I decided to spend it revisiting and entering the Great Pyramid. I took a bus to the ticket booth and bought a ticket. I walked toward the entrance, passing several young men riding camels. The entrance was such a small door that I had to crawl up a ladder to get in. Then I had to walk up the stairs that were lit by bulbs. It was cool inside. I could see long hallways to other parts of the monument, but they were roped off. I was all alone without a tour guide. I eventually reached the top and entered a room with a large box. I expected to see a mummy, but it had nothing but a tombstone. I stayed there for a while meditating on the Black people who were there thousands of years ago. Then in the complete silence, I suddenly felt afraid until some Japanese people came into the room. I went back down the stairs and left the interior of the Great Pyramid. I walked around it and saw the two more pyramids that I had seen before not too far away. They were smaller than the one I had just left. I continued to walk to the Sphinx where some men were evidently doing some construction or maintenance work. I sat down near the feet of the Sphinx and watched for a few minutes, imagining myself back in ancient times. Finally, I walked back to the bus that would take me back to the hotel. As I rode, the words of a Negro spiritual came to mind: "Go down, Moses, way down in Egypt land; tell old Pharaoh to let my people go." I thanked God and my ancestors for the opportunity to see for myself this cradle of the world's Black civilization.

CHAPTER 26

Return to Houston

Back in Detroit, I kept thinking about Kharisma. I wanted to call her but couldn't find her phone number. But on Easter Sunday 1996, while I was in the dining room having dinner, Lieutenant Adisa, who was from Houston, came in and told me I had a phone call. When I answered, I was delighted to find that it was Kharisma. "I missed you," she said. "Why haven't you called me?" I explained that I had lost her number. She asked me if I was in a relationship and I assured her that I wasn't. "I want to see you. When are you coming back?" she asked. "As soon as I can," I said. "I want to see you, too." For months we talked on the phone almost every night. The more we talked the more certain I was that she was the woman I wanted to spend the rest of my life with. While I was in Egypt, I decided that I was ready to move back to the South, and since Kharisma lived in Houston, it might as well be there.

Every time I sat in a car for a long time, I was in a lot of pain, so I was no longer traveling as a missionary for the church. I got a job working for Mel Farr, the famous Black running back for the Detroit Lions from 1967 -1973 he became a business owner for Ford dealership. Bishop Kehinde got his brother Floyd the night supervisor to give me a job at the dealership cleaning up the shop at night. When I had saved enough money, I took a weekend trip to Houston. Cardinal Mbiyu met me at the airport and drove me to Kharisma's house; we greeted each other warmly. I expected to spend the night with her, but her sons would be at home that night and she was not yet ready for them to meet me. They were supposed to be with their father that weekend, but for some reason he was unable to keep them. So, after a wonderful meal that she had prepared for me, Cardinal Myibu came back and took me to his apartment. She was so busy with her sons all weekend that our time together was limited. After my return to Detroit, we continued to talk on the phone. Part of me wanted to stay in Detroit, but love was calling me to Houston. I continued to work and save my money. By the Sunday before Christmas, I had saved enough to move, and Cardinal Baye informed the congregation that I was transferring my membership to Shrine Number 10 in Houston, Texas. He had me stand to loud clapping from the congregation. It was a very emotional moment for me. After the service I received many hugs and well wishes. But there was a deep sadness, too. Captain Cheo had become sick and was walking on a cane. He was very ill but had managed to make it to church to wish me farewell. He said, "Dadisi, that trip to the Bahamas was the best trip I ever had. Thank you." I told him that, God willing, when I saved some money, we would go again, but I think we both knew that, in his condition, that would never happen. The next day I said goodbye to all my friends whom I hadn't already seen. I went to Mother Naomi's house to tell her how much she had helped me as a poet and writer and as a wonderful friend. We promised to stay in touch.

When Bishop Badilifu drove me to the airport, a snow storm was raging. When I arrived in Houston it seemed like a different world. The sun was shining brightly, and the weather was more like spring than winter. I swore I would never live in the North again.

Kharisma picked me up from Hobby Airport. She had her sons, Thomas and Keith with her. I was seeing them for the first time. When she introduced them, I told them I had heard great things about them and their performance in school. They had evidently heard about me too and seemed happy to meet me. After picking up my luggage we drove to her house. The next day was Christmas. After breakfast we drove to the Shrine for services. When we were walking from the parked car I was surprised to see my friend Imara from Detroit. Without as much as a simple greeting she told me that Captain Cheo had just died. I didn't want to believe it, but I knew it was true; I just didn't expect it so soon. I told Kharisma and the boys to go on into the church and I would join them soon. I didn't want to break down in their presence. I could hardly make it into the men's restroom before the tears began to gush in grief for the friend and brother I had lost. Whenever I was broke, he would lend me money. When I needed someone to talk to he was also there to listen. Eventually I pulled myself together enough to go into the sanctuary and greeted some friends I already knew and met others who were new to me.

After the service we went back to Kharisma's house where we exchanged gifts. In the presence of the boys, I got down on my knees and asked Kharisma to marry me. She said she would. It should have been a happy occasion, but it was marred by the loss of my friend and the fact that my remaining funds were so limited that I could not afford to go back to Detroit for his funeral.

Living in a new city and having a ready-made family required that I think of *we* more than *me*. For a long time, we all got along fine. During the holiday season we would get up early and go walking to the neighborhood park. Then we would come back home for breakfast. The boys, ten and eleven years old, were still excited about their games and toys. After breakfast they would go to their room to play while Kharisma and I watched television. Some evenings we dressed in our African attire and went to the community center to celebrate Kwaanza; there I was introduced to some of her friends. After the new year began, we sat down and discussed which one of us would be responsible for which household expenses. We decided not to rush into marriage until I got a steady job.

Each morning I would read the want ads in the paper. In Detroit I had once worked part time delivering pizza, so I took a bus downtown to apply for a job at a Pizza Parlor until I could find something better. There was indeed an opening, but it was in the evening and I would have to ride a bike to make deliveries to the downtown office buildings. After giving it some thought, I decided against it. For the last nine years I had worked as a printer and hoped to find employment in that field, but time went by and I still hadn't found work.

Every other weekend the boys would visit their father, and Kharisma and I were left alone. Gradually I noticed a change in her attitude. I knew she needed time to prepare her lesson plans for school and I would leave her alone when she was busy. But I found that when we were alone together, we had little to talk about, and too often when we did talk, she complained about something I had or had not done. The newness of living together was wearing off and I began to wonder if we were really in love and if we married, what kind of marriage it would be. By the end of February, I still hadn't found a job, and Kharisma seemed to be more and more impatient with my presence.

One morning she woke me up screaming that I had eaten the boys' breakfast. I didn't know what she was talking about. She said, "The two eggs and bacon."

I replied that I didn't know that there was no more. "Why didn't you tell me last night? I could have gone to the store and bought some more."

"You should have known," she snapped. "Don't ever do that again."

That Friday evening when Kharisma came home she did not speak to me. She got up and left the house early that Saturday morning without saying a word to me. When she got home late that night, I asked her where she had been. She just said, "Out with some friends." Two nights later when I was lying in the bed, Kharisma walked into the room with an angry look on her face. She told me she needed to talk to me. "I'm listening," I said.

She asked, "Are you going to marry me or not?"

"Not the way things are with your attitude."

"Well, you need to get the hell out of my house," she yelled. "By tomorrow." She stormed out of the room slamming the door behind her. I agreed that it was best that I leave. Since she had never been married, I wondered if she had ever loved me or just wanted a husband—any husband. The next morning after Kharisma went to school, I got dressed and went to the Shrine's residence hall and told Captain Alimayu about my predicament. He said he had an extra room in his apartment and I was welcome to stay with him. He loaned me his car so that I could go back to get all my belongings. Sometimes I would see Kharisma at church and we would speak politely, but nothing more.

As the years went by I did find employment and was able to sustain myself. One Sunday after the service, Kharisma stopped me and asked why I didn't attend any of the evening functions at church. I told her I didn't have time because I was working two jobs. As she was walking away, she turned around and said, "You're a good man. I should have kept you."

CHAPTER 27

At Last

During the eleven years after I asked Kharisma to marry me, I was involved in a few relationships but nothing serious. However, in May 2007, when I was in a grocery store shopping for lunch I saw a very attractive Black woman whom I wanted to meet. I will call her Rosalind. I followed her as she went from aisle to aisle, and suddenly I was standing next to her. After some small talk about the selections of bread, I introduced myself.

She said, "It's nice to meet you. My name is Rosalind."

"You're very attractive; I'm single and I'd like to get to know you. Would you mind if I call you sometime?"

She said she was single but very busy with schoolwork. "I wouldn't take much of your time," I said.

She looked at me for a long time, then said, "Give me *your* number and I'll call *you* when I have time."

"Fair enough," I said. I took a pen and a piece of paper from my pocket and wrote my name and phone number on it and gave it to her. We shook hands and went our separate ways. After waiting for a couple of weeks, I concluded that she never had any intention of calling me and gave up hope. A year passed and I forgot about her. I often shopped at the same grocery store but didn't see her again.

Then one day I was in the checkout line behind a woman. A Black female clerk was bagging the lady's grocery in front of me. The clerk happened to look up at me. "Don't I know you from somewhere?"

I looked at her for a long time and finally recognized her as Rosalind. "Yes, we met in this same store a long time ago and I gave you my phone number."

When I told her my name, she said, "Now I remember. Call me tonight. Here's my phone number."

I called her that night and she seemed happy to hear from me. We must have talked until midnight about her and my past relationships. She said she hadn't called me because her last relationship had ended badly and she didn't want to be hurt again. We agreed to meet for lunch the next day.

The next day I arrived at the restaurant before she did. It was crowded and we had to wait a long time for a table. We spent the time talking and getting to know each other better. Eventually we were seated and enjoyed a delightful meal. Even after the meal we continued to talk. Then I walked her to her car. "Call me," she said. "We'll talk some more." I called her for the next few nights and felt that I was really getting to know her. I liked her better with each conversation. She seemed to have all the qualities I admired in a woman.

A few days later after church on Sunday, I went to the same grocery store where I usually shopped and Warren, a church friend was with me. I ran into Rosalind again. I introduced her to Warren. She said that she would be getting off work soon.

"What are you doing today?" I asked, would you like to come to my place for dinner this evening? We can go to a movie afterward."

I'll call you and let you know," she said. We shook hands. She went back to work and I continued shopping. Shortly before I started cooking, she called and said she wasn't hungry but would love to go to a movie with me. I gave her directions to my house. She promised to come to my place after I had finished eating. When she arrived Warren and I had just finished eating. I had promised to take Warren home after dinner. He was drinking some wine. I offered her a glass, but she said, "No thanks."

We got in my car to take Warren home, and Rosalind decided to sit in the back seat. This was the first time going to Warren's residence and didn't realize he lived so far on the North side of town. After the long drive Rosalind and I decided not to go to the movie. Instead, she wanted to show me her garden in the front of her house. She had a beautiful garden with all kinds of flowers. We sat in my car and talked for a while before I gave her a hug and went home.

◆ ◆ ◆

After being trained as a dialysis technician, I worked in a clinic with patients who came in three times a week for dialysis. I liked the job and the fact that I was helping people whose kidneys were not functioning properly. I also got to meet some interesting people who would tell me about their lives. I considered them as friends. I also got to know one of my co-workers,

Yolanda. Between patients we talked about our lives. She knew that I was very fond of Rosalind whom I had been dating exclusively now for a week.

"When are you going to propose to her," she asked me one day. "From all you've told me about your feelings, I think you're deeply in love with her." I was speechless. For the first time I admitted to myself that I was indeed in love with her. Perhaps I hadn't asked her to marry me because I was afraid that she would turn me down.

"You'll never know until you ask her," she replied.

One evening shortly after my conversation with Yolanda, I got the nerves to call Rosalind and ask her to come to my place. "I have something I need to ask you," I said.

Without an explanation, she said, "I'll be right over." She was there in no time. After a few pleasantries, I said, "I know I haven't known you very long, but I know enough about you to be sure that you are the woman I want to spend the rest of my life with. Will you marry me?" I was surprised and happy when she answered quickly.

"Yes," she said. "I feel the same way about you. I was hoping you would ask me." We kissed passionately.

"I want to get married on my mother's birthday, August 9," she said. "That's about a month and a half away, but I'm not interested in having a big wedding. My first marriage ended in divorce."

I explained that I wanted a big enough wedding to have all my large family present because this would be my first and last marriage ceremony. She agreed.

The following Monday we went downtown to the courthouse to get the marriage license. Later that evening we went to the jewelry store shop for rings. I notified all my family members and asked them to come to Houston to witness my marriage. The wedding we planned would include a lot of guests but would be a simple ceremony. The ceremony would be at the Shrine of the Black Madonna, of course. Rosalind asked her sister Debra to be her bridesmaid; her brother Melvin would walk her down the aisle and give her away. I selected my brother Clifford to be my best man. My good friend, Cardinal Mbiyu Chui would marry us.

The time went by quickly and soon our wedding day arrived. Everyone in my family came for this major event in my life. My mother was in the beginning stages of Alzheimer's. I don't think she was fully aware of what was going on, but she came anyhow. At five o'clock the service began with a recording of Etta James singing "At Last" as Rosalind and her brother walked down the aisle. She looked so beautiful in her wedding dress! After Clifford and I followed them to the front, I surprised her by singing "This Magic Moment," by The Drifters.

After that, everything went as we had planned. When the minister said, "You may now kiss the bride," I knew we were beginning a wonderful new life together as a married couple. As we walked down the aisle, the words of the song rang in my ear. "At last my love has come along. My lonely days are over and life is like a song." A wonderful new phase of my life was now beginning.

CHAPTER 28

Married Life

Rosalind and I did not go on a honeymoon. The monetary gifts we received were used to pay for the wedding. In addition, we were living in the house that Rosalind was already buying. I took over the mortgage and Rosalind and I paid half of the utility bills. I felt that once the mortgage was paid off we could sell that house and buy a larger one, but Rosalind didn't want to sell the house. She wanted to give it to her son. She seemed to ignore the contributions I was making and thought more of her son's rights than mine. We had been married only three months and already there were serious disagreements. Rosalind knew how to cook but didn't like to. Instead, we went out to eat often. When she did choose to cook, she would cook a large pot of something that I didn't particularly like and it would last for two or three days. I was glad that I knew how to cook for myself. Some evenings we would sit on the front porch and talk about our lives before we met. I always listened patiently to her stories, but when I told mine, she showed little or no interest. Our religious backgrounds were different. She was raised in the Lutheran Church; I was a Black Christian Nationalist who believed that Jesus came to liberate the Black Nation Israel from white Gentile oppression. Although she still attended her own church, she joined the Shrine with me. I truly loved Rosalind and was grateful that she paid all our bills on time. Also, she was very handy. She could fix things around the house that I had no idea how to fix. I was better at housecleaning. Sometimes I tried to help, but she refused my help. When she got mad at me, she would complain that I never helped her do anything.

I replied, "You never asked for my help."

"I shouldn't have to. You can see for yourself that burned out light bulb needs to be replaced."

Rosalind and I separated several times during our troubled marriage. I realize now that if we had discussed our problems these separations might have been avoided. When she did discuss her complaints they would be about something of which I was unaware. Then she would bring up other things that had nothing to do with the original complaint. Sometimes I felt pushed to the limit. For months at a time I would leave and stay with an older woman who was like a mother to me. Once I rented my own apartment. Still we were not completely separated. Sometimes I would go back home or she would come and stay with me in my apartment. She was sweet to me when we were not living together. Eventually I gave up my apartment and moved back home hoping things would improve. For a while they did. Then she started complaining that I was spending too much time developing myself as a DJ and artist and not working on our relationship. Things became very cool. It was obvious that we were going in two different directions. Sometimes when her son or granddaughters were involved in an event, I could not attend because I was earning extra money driving part time for Uber. After two nights of arguing, I gave up. She asked me why I had married her. I told her I loved her, but I could not deal with all the endless arguments. I began to realize that this marriage just couldn't work and I decided to leave and get a divorce. There was no point in staying in a marriage where both of us were unhappy.

CHAPTER 29

From Then to Now

After the breakup of my marriage, it was my intention to move back home to Charleston. In fact, I did make three trips back, but with each trip I became less sure that leaving Houston would be a good idea. Many changes had taken place with my family members. My brother Eddie had committed suicide in 1983. My little sister Izetta had died from a drug overdose in 1998. My father had died of a heart attack on January 2, 1999. Later that year my oldest brother "Wonnie" died of health issues, leaving behind his wife, Betty and their four sons. Nothing could ever be the same as it used to be.

My brother Clifford still lives in Atlantic City, New Jersey with his wife, Barbara and their children. He fulfilled his promised to our mother by getting his GED and becoming the only child to go to college and get an Associate degree in Accounting. Clarissa and Mamie are both married and still living in Charleston. In 2017, Annette became a widow and is now living with her daughter Stephanie in Myrtle Beach, South Caroline. My mother lived in a nursing home for seven years. However, in May of 2017 my sisters decided to take her back to her own home. She is now 90 years old and suffers with Alzheimer's. Miriam's husband, Mack died, and she lives with her and takes care of Mother, with the help of my other sisters; they take turns helping out every night.

In addition to family changes, I realized that whenever I went back home I rarely saw any of my old friends, except for Larry Polite, Spencer (Ace), who now goes by his Muslim name, Hamid, and my dear friend Oleather Smith. Bogard Street is no longer Black anymore. White folk have moved in the neighborhood.

Furthermore, Charleston is a small town compared to Houston. There are fewer places to go and things to do. Houston is a far more exciting place to live and I have had much better jobs than I would have been able to find at home. It was not difficult for me to decide to stay in Houston for the present. I am still very strongly involved with the Shrine of the Black Madonna. In 2019, I retired from the Maccabees after forty years of service.

The Founder of the Shrines of the Black Madonna of the Pan African Orthodox Christian Church, Rev. Albert B. Cleage Jr., who renamed himself Jaramogi Abebe Agyeman died in his sleep at the age of 88 on February 20, 2002 while visiting Beulah Land, our church farm in Calhoun Falls, South Carolina. His legacy will live on by the work of our church members. The Beulah Land farm has over 4,000 acres of land. Making it the largest Black owned farmland in North America. The Shrine has a new Presiding Bishop, Jaramogi Menelik Kimathi Nelson whom we love and wish the best. The Shrine has also expanded to the continent of Africa with churches in Monrovia, Liberia.

Over the years my life has continue to evolve. At one time I worked for a medical company as a laboratory technician building equipment for doctors to use in performing heart surgery. After hours, I drove for Uber part time. Eventually I was one of the workers at the medical company who got laid off when the company was downsizing and Uber was the only job I had. It paid well, but not enough. I needed to find another full-time job.

One day in March 2018, I received an email from one of my friends, Charlotte Hawkins, who I once worked with at a medical company asking me if I was still looking for a job. She had been informed that the pharmaceutical company that presently employed her had an opening for a production technician and she suggested that I go to their web site and download their application, fill it out, and send it in with my resume, using her name as a reference. I followed her instructions. That Tuesday I received a call from an employee there named Meagan Copper who had received my material and asked me several questions, which I answered to the best of my ability. She was evidently satisfied because she asked me to come to the office in Sugarland, Texas (about a half hour from home) for a personal interview at two o'clock Thursday, two days later.

I arrived a half-hour early and was greeted by Ms. Copper, who was Black. She led me to a small room and told me someone would see me in a few minutes. Moments later an Hispanic lady entered and introduced herself as Mrs. Hernandez, the production technician supervisor. She asked me to tell her about my work experience in the medical field for the last twenty years. I told her about all the jobs that I had listed on my resume. She seemed pleased with my experience and said someone would contact me soon. Two days later, Ms. Copper called and offered me the job. My job would be to inspect the drugs in their containers and package them for shipment. She told me what my salary would be. The pay sounded very good and I was happy to accept the job offer.

◆ ◆ ◆

As of this writing, I am 60 years old. I have always wanted to go back to Africa and am saving money for such a trip. My main interest this time is

Mount Kilimanjaro. My female friend is from Tanzania and she wants to take me to her country and visit the mountain of my dreams.

During my early years, the ministers and teachers of the Shrine of the Black Madonna taught me a great deal about African history that prepared me for what was to come. Going to Egypt was one of the main highlights of my life. Seeing and touching ancient monuments that my African ancestors built was truly astonishing. Even though my trips to Africa were many years ago, I still have fond memories of the continent. I have been blessed to be able to visit many other parts of the world, meeting some fascinating people along the way.

Life has taught me to love myself, despite all my flaws, and to learn from and forgive myself for all the mistakes I have made. I know that I am a child of God, and nothing God created is inferior. I believe that we were born to grow spiritually and educationally and become better persons from year to year. I also believe that God intended my life to be a good example for others and to serve humanity.

When I look back on my early life and remember that little boy who had difficulty learning how to read and write, it amazes me that my strongest goal even then was to be a writer, the skill at which I was least prepared. Writing has been a long 34-year uphill struggle, but the Spirit of God through the Shrine has kept preparing me for better things to come. It seems impossible that that illiterate special education student has to date self-published seven books and two CDs, but with God, all things are possible.

After taking the time to look back and fully digest all of my experiences, I decided on April 15, 1984 that it was time to begin writing my autobiography, adding to it as more events occur. This book is the result of that decision. Although I hope to live many more years, something told me that I should end it at this point, even if that decision later requires a second book that will continue where this one ends.

My story reminds me of the Negro spiritual, "We are climbing Jacob's ladder . . . . Every round goes higher 'n' higher. . . ." My life has indeed been an upward road and with God's help, I intend to keep on climbing.

Dadisi Mwende Netifnet
" 2002 Poet of the Year Award", Orlando, FL

Anna Mae and Elijah Alston, Parents

Dadisi, The Boy

From left to right-Aunt Grace,
Greatgrandmother Mamie J. Simmons
and Grandmother Mother Eva.
Picture taken in 1971

Bottom Row: Left to right: Dadisi; Anna Mae (mother); Niece, Yolanda;
Elijah(father); **Second Row**: Left to right: Annette; Izetta, Betty (sister-in-law);
Baby Elijah; Alston, III; Clarissa (sister); **Top Row:** Left to right: Miriam,
Wonnie; and Mamie.

My mother and her 6 children. From left to right Miriam, Clifford, me,
Annette, Mother, Clarissa and Mamie.

Some members of the Family

Sister, Clarissa, Dadisi & Mother

My Childhood Best friends;
Larry and Spencer (Ace)

The Slave Market Museum
6 Chalmers St. Charleston, SC

Dadisi in Egypt, 1996

Book signing event

Book signing supporters
Shrine Cultural Center, Houston, TX

1822 Freedom fighter Denmark Vessey
Statue Hampark Park, Charleston, SC

Gambia West Africa

Dadisi, Gambia, West Africa, 1994

Dadisi and Nikki Giovanni
Shrine Cultural Center, Houston TX

Maya Angelou, Eugene B Redmond, Dadisi & students.
Oakland University, Detroit 1993

Dadisi in the Great Pyramid of Giza

The Great Pyramid of Giza, Egypt

Senegal, West Africa trip, 1994

Schomburg Center for Research in Black Culture, Harlem
Delegates going to West Africa, 1994
Sponsored by McDonald's/WMXD Radio in Detroit, MI

Dadisi, Washington DC., White House

Dadisi in Washington, DC, Marine Corps War Memorial

Honor guards Maccabees at the home going service for Mother Soyini.
From left to right Lt. Kokayi, Sgt. Tarik, Lt. Xolani, Major Bambaata,
Lt. Nantambu, myself and Major Sundiata.

From left to right myself Lt. Xolani, Lt. Nantambu, Gen.Chui, Capt. Teketeke,
Col. Kalomo, Sgt. Tarik. Top row from right to left Capt. Badilifu, Col. Taha,
Major Sundiata and Gen.Zizwe

My brother and best friend Edward
(Gus) Alston. Gone too soon.
I missed him so much.

Reverend Aswad Walker and I in the
Shrine parking lot. He too is a writer.

Pictured center: Senegalese historian, Dr. Cheikh Anta Diop;
me on the end, right. 1985 (My apology for not recollecting names
of others in the photo)

Maccabee Kehinda and his wife Tiombe. Kehinda drove me from Atlanta to Detroit in 1986.

This is brother Adande and I in Atlanta on May 12, 2019. In 1985 he was my roommate at the Shrine. He would take me to his job on the weekends and have me copy my manuscript "Poetry For Today's Young Black Revolutionary Minds" to be sent out to publishers. It got published in 1994.

Cardinal Sondai K. Lester and wife Cardinal Lindiwe.
They taught me how to become a Black Christian Nationalist. They both have since retired from the ministry.
Thank you for your services.

Uwinmana- My Lifelong Sister

Late Mrs. Barbara Martin (Cardinal Nandi) She was The National Director of The Shrine of the Black Madonna Cultural Center and Bookstores. I missed her so much.

Alemu and his wife, Miata Foluke. I have known them for 40 years. Alemu is like my brother from another mother

Jaramogi Abebe Agyeman Holy Patriarch and Founder of the Shrine of the Black Madonna. The church that he built saved my life. I am forever greatful to him.

Reverend Diallo, Trained me to be a printer in Detroit

Dadisi, Rev. Hawiyah, Mother Defina, Lt. Kokayi

Left to right, members from Shrine 10, Houston, TX:
Rev. Kazi, Makeda, Njemile, Olaniyi and I

Left to Right: Sanyika, me, General Zizwe, Jaramogi
Kimathi, Lt. Kokayi, Rev. Djenaba and Runako

Uncle Felix and Aunt Grace Christian
I visited them in New York City in
1976. They are also my Godparents.

My Detroit Vita Sasa Group

GENERAL MASAI BOLOGUN

Co-founder of the Shrine
of the Black Madonna
Maccabees

In loving memory of
PM Clifford Erving Alston, Jr.
May 10, 1970 - April 22, 2019

My nephew "Slugger"
In Memory, April 22, 2019

One of the many groups that I function with
in Atlanta. Corporal Tacuma on the far right
gave me my first tour of shrine 9.

Mwalimu Sekou and his wife
Fundi Morenike were my first
assistants group leaders when
I joined shrine 9 in 1978.

Corporal Adisa was with me
at McDonald's restaurant
when we both filled out a
form to win a trip to West
Africa in 1994.

I was Bishop Mbiyu best man when he got
married to Binta in Atlanta.

205

Naomi Long Madgett - Poet Mother.
Poet Laureate of Detroit

Naomi Long Madgett, Ph. D.

October 12, 2012

Dadisi, my dear son,

As always, it was so good to talk to you the other day. I always enjoy hearing from you and learning of your latest project, but I do miss you very much and recall the years when you were in Detroit and we could communicate in person. You were helpful to me in so many ways and when you left, I wondered how I would ever get along without you.

I am extremely proud of what you have made of yourself—your published works and your work in progress. You are a wonderful role model and inspiration to younger aspiring writers who are encouraged by reading your books. But that is not the only way that you have been a good role model, especially to young African American men who, unfortunately, don't have enough moral Christian men of good character to pattern themselves after. In my own life, I have found that someone is watching me all the time whether I know it or not and many will be influenced by the way I speak, the respect I show others, the way I carry myself, my character. I owe it to all of them to lead them in the right direction by my own behavior. It makes me very proud that you are following my example, and I am so very, very proud of you. It gives me great pleasure to hear you call me Mother and to own you as the son I never had. If I had ever had a biological son, I would have wanted him to be just like you.

At the age of ninety, I find myself reviewing my life and deciding what to keep and what to throw away.

Ever since I have known you, our relationship has been among my blessings and my most positive experiences.

You have my love and all good wishes for your continued success.

Naomi Long Madgett, Ph.D.

Poet Laureate, City of Detroit

MEMORABLE
LETTERS AND DOCUMENTS

My inauguration gifts to President Obama on his second term as President at the White House United States January 21 2013

WASHINGTON, DC 20500

$000.46

Dadisi Netifnet
Apartment 3
3921 Omear Drive
Houston, Texas 77025

I recieved this letter on April 4, 2013 the
45th Anniversary of the assassination of
Dr. Martin Luther King Jr. Poet Dadisi mn Netifnet

THE WHITE HOUSE
WASHINGTON

We would like to extend our deepest thanks and appreciation for
your generous gift.

It is gratifying to know that we have your support. As we work to
address the great challenges of our time, we hope you will continue to
stay active and involved.

Again, thank you for your kind gift.

Barack Obama   Michelle Obama

WWW.WHITEHOUSE.GOV

My gifts to the President and First Lady
were my two books "Love Flows Like A
River" and "Think With Your Spiritual Mind"
I also send them a copy of my new
cd "I Saw Two Rainbows In The Sky"

Continental
Cablevision

March 7, 1994

Dadisi Metilnet
760 Seward #306
Detroit, MI 48202

Dear Mr. Metilnet:

Enclosed is a copy of the "1994 African American Read-In" program
that you participated in. I really appreciate you taking the time
to perform for us. Your performance was definitely a highlight of
the program.

Thanks again!

Sincerely,

Christina Coppola
Producer–Continental Cablevision

Detroit, Michigan

27600 Franklin Road • Southfield, Michigan 48034 • Telephone (313) 355-3906

April 22, 2004

Dr. William "Bill" Cosby
P.O. Box 4840
Santa Monica, California 90411

Dear Dr. Cosby:

First let me introduce myself. I am Dadisi Mwende Netifnet, a/k/a Marvin LeRoy Abron. I am a member of the Shrine of the Black Madonna of the Pan-African Orthodox Christian Church, founded by Dr. Albert B. Cleage. I am a struggling poet and author, who has self-published several books and received many community and national awards for my work.

I am currently celebrating my 20th anniversary as a writer and I would like to share my joy with those who have inspired and motivated me over the years. I am giving you these autographed copies of my books because your achievements as an artist and an educator have motivated me to continue to grow and to always do my best. Each one has been a great labor of love as well as an accomplishment that many felt I would never achieve. I also have a novel and an autobiography in the works. You see, I was an adult when I learned to read and write. It was not until I joined the Shrine as a young adult that anyone saw the possibilities in me and gave me a sense of who I really was, not who people said I was (many of whom were teachers). I found my faith and I kept believing in God and myself as I worked to accomplish one of my many goals in life.

Now it is time to take it to the next level. As a self-published author, my volume of books is very limited and therefore my focus must be directed to the most productive methods of distribution. If you enjoy my books, would you help me by introducing them to an agent or a publisher? I will continue to struggle to get the doors opened and I believe that I have something worthy of the public. But we know that many times it is not how good a project is but who introduces it or takes note of it that can make or break it. I do believe in Divine Order, and the word of God says, we have not because we ask not, so I am asking. Thank you for your time and your consideration. Best wishes also to your wife Camille and your family.

Sincerely,

Dadisi Mwende Netifnet

1608 MARTIN LUTHER KING BLVD. APT. 37 • HOUSTON, TX • 77021
PHONE: 832.498.7614 • FAX: 713.441.6897

THE LIBRARY OF CONGRESS
WASHINGTON, D.C. 20540

POETRY AND LITERATURE CENTER

October 4, 1993

Dear Dadisi Mwende Netifnet:

Thank you very much for your book, Poetry for Today's Young Black
Revolutionary Minds, which was waiting for me as I took up my duties as Poet Laureate this
fall. I look forward to reading it.

With best wishes,

Rita Dove

Rita Dove
Poet Laureate

Mr. Dadisi Mwende Netifnet
700 Seward
#306
Detroit, MI 48202

Dear Oprah Winfrey,   May 24, 2006

I have been watching your television show for years. As an African American male I am so very proud of you and how you spend your celebrity life here on God's earth trying to make it a better place for mankind. In April 2006 I was watching your television show special on the GENOCIDE that has been taking place in Darfur, Sudan. I cried throughout the entire show. Thank God your show empowered me as to what I could do to help bring about a change in Sudan.
As a result, I wrote two letters to my Senators from Texas asking them of their views on what's going on in Sudan, how they could help and to please help Senator Obama with humanitarian aids to this crisis to Africa. Not only that, I started a petition and collected 85 signatures on that same day so that our Senators in Texas would realize how much this matter to me. Thank you for bringing some light to our motherland Africa.

Oprah, I have written four books three poetry books and one humorous book. One of my WILDEST DREAM is to see my books publish by a major publishing company. I am a struggling self-published author. Nothing would be so gratifying to me than to walk into a bookstore and see one of my books on a bookshelf. Now that would be my WILDEST DREAM. Please let me know if I could send my books to you as a gift. Keep up the good fight my beautiful sister and may God's spirit continue to shine though you.

Peace and love,

Poet Dadisi

April 11, 2011

Dear Dadisi, you have put pen to paper and allowed us to grow with you as you developed your talent and expressed your views and feelings as a Black man in America. As I read your poems and prose, I could feel what you felt and remember what it felt like for me as a child of the Civil Rights Era.

Thank you for caring enough to listen to God when he placed the words in your head and having the heart to write it down to be shared by others who need to know what faith can do for you. You are an inspiration to all who come into contact with you. I pray that you will never lose your zest for life...that you will keep writing...and that you will never, ever, get too busy to hear the voice of God.

Yours in the struggle
Dr. Evelyn Serwa Bethune
Granddaughter of Dr. Mary McLeod Bethune

Famous Poets Master Workshop

Diploma

Is Hereby Awarded to Famous Poet for 2002

Dadisi Mwende Netifnet

Honored Recipient of the Shakespeare Trophy of Excellence
And 2002 Poet of the Year Medallion

For Successfully Completing FAMOUS POETS MASTER WORKSHOP[c]
"The Spoken Word: Techniques for Giving Voice to Your Poetry"
Personally Conducted by the Eminent Actor & Director Al D'Andrea

Famous Poets Eighth Annual Poetry Convention
The Wyndham Palace • Orlando, Florida • Aug. 31 – Sept. 2, 2002
Presented Under the Auspices of
Famous Poets Institute for Advanced Poetical Studies™

Mark Schramm, *Executive Director*   Al D'Andrea, *Master Workshop Conductor*

ABOUT THE AUTHOR

Dadisi Mwende Netifnet, born Marvin Leroy Alston, in Charleston, South Carolina. Through the years, he has been in an intense struggle to improve his art of writing. He has read his poetry in many cities throughout the United States and Canada. He has also read his poetry in many different countries throughout the world, such as: Egypt, Senegal, Gambia and Freeport, Grand Bahamas. In 2002, Dadisi was awarded the Shakespeare Trophy of Excellence and the 2002 Poet of the Year Gold Medallion by the Famous Poets Society. Dadisi resides in Houston, Texas. Look for him at area poetry readings, arrange for him to read to your group, or get one or all of his publications for your library. You will be uplifted and delighted.